Descartes and Foucault

A Contrastive Introduction to Philosophy

Descartes and Foucault

A Contrastive Introduction to Philosophy

C. G. Prado

University of Ottawa Press

© University of Ottawa Press, 1992
Printed and bound in Canada
ISBN 0-7766-0275-6

Canadian Cataloguing in Publication Data

Prado, C. G.
Descartes and Foucault

Includes bibliographical references and index.
ISBN 0-7766-0275-6

1. Descartes, René, 1596-1650. Meditationes de prima
philosophia. 2. Foucault, Michel. Histoire de la sexualité.
3. Knowledge, Theory of. I. Title.

B1854.P72 1992   121   C92-090190-5

Cover design by Robert Dolbec

CONTENTS

INTRODUCTION

PREFATORY REMARKS

THIS BOOK is about an enterprise which Plato (428–348 B.C.) saw as a holy quest and Friedrich Wilhelm Nietzsche (1844–1900) saw as a malignant obsession: the search for absolute truth and achievement of unconditional knowledge. As such this book is about the very heart of philosophizing. In what follows my main objective is to introduce philosophy to the novice by contrasting the most radically opposed traditional and critical contemporary views on the quest for truth and knowledge, the former deriving from Plato and the latter from Nietzsche. My secondary objective is to characterize, for those already familiar with traditional philosophy, the critical contemporary side of these hugely divergent positions on knowledge and truth. The view or perspective I contrast with traditional philosophy, particularly received Anglo-American philosophical orthodoxy, is that which presently poses the sharpest challenge to that orthodoxy, but which too often is perceived by mainstream philosophers as inaccessible because it derives from an unfamiliar "Continental" tradition and is usually couched in what they perceive as an alien idiom.

Most of what I say below by way of asides, clarifications and amplifications, and advice to the reader is directed to the novice, but I have tried to present the material in a way which will engage both the novice and those more knowledgeable about philosophy. In this connection, I should acknowledge that the text may sometimes appear repetitious. The reason for this is that the elusiveness of many of the points to be made requires that I come at them from different sides and in different ways. Additionally, the aim is always primarily to convey perspectives and modes of thinking about something, rather than sheer information. And with respect to what may seem repetitious, I strongly advise the more knowledgeable reader not to skip Part I. Whether it presents new or familiar material, Part I provides a necessary backdrop to Part II. The most common error, made even by the most knowledgeable, with respect to understanding contemporary challenges to traditional philosophy is too hastily to assume understanding of precisely what it is that is challenged. Part I not only introduces the novice to traditional philosophy, it also provides the expert with an explicit account of what is now seen as most problematic in traditional philosophy.

As an introduction to philosophy my project is very unconventional, both because of its contrastive approach, which gives equal weight to traditional and antithetic positions, and because standard introductory texts tend either to tell only Plato's side or to emphasize it heavily. When Nietzsche's side is given, it is too often painted as at best a productive challenge to the mainstream or at worst only a provocative and unworkable extreme. The tendency is to characterize Plato's views as paradigmatic of philosophy as objective, reasoned inquiry, and Nietzsche's views as too subjectivistic and basically contrary, and somehow as just too exuberant to define mainstream philosophy. There is some truth in this, for in spite of the intrinsic value of his work, in the history of philosophy Nietzsche seems most effective as a counterpoint to Plato, and his epigrammatic and provocative style does reflect thought of an intensity and heat not often associated with the cool reasoning taken as characteristic of philosophy. Moreover, if mainstream philosophy were Nietzschean in character, Plato would be the iconoclast, and his rigorous and judicious reasoning would provide the counterpoint to Nietzschean exuberance. Nonetheless, because the Platonic is the dominant tradition, for too long philosophy has been presented to the novice not only as characterized by the detached Platonic search for truth and knowledge, but as *defined* by it, and so as largely monolithic in spirit and method, if not in doctrinal detail.

The writing of this book was prompted by the realization that an introduction to philosophy can no longer be a one-sided exposition of a philosophical tradition which Alfred North Whitehead (1861–1947) once described as a series of footnotes to Plato. If only because of recent critiques of traditional philosophical methods and assumptions, it is now necessary, when introducing people to the discipline, to alert them to the debate about the consistency and clarity of the traditional conceptions of truth, of knowledge, of intellectual inquiry, and so about the very possibility of traditional philosophy. I see this as a very positive requirement, because a beginner could not hope for a more challenging introduction to a discipline than one which asks whether that discipline is itself possible as a productive intellectual enterprise. As for the more knowledgeable, little could be more demanding, and thus intellectually productive, than to come to grips with the claim that what they are knowledgeable *about* is inherently misconceived.

What follows is a topic-focused introduction to philosophy, or perhaps to how philosophy might be reconceived. In either case what this book relies on is detailed discussion of limited subject matter to provide representative coverage. Most introductory texts try for comprehensive coverage of the entire discipline, but in doing so they invariably leave the beginner with a mass of information and little idea of how to organize or use it. In particular, introductory texts tend to leave the novice without much sense of priorities in philosophy. This book will introduce the reader to philosophy, or to how philosophy has been rethought, by focusing on just two philosophers and their definitive work in philosophy's single most central area of inquiry: epistemology, or the theory of knowledge. The aim is to familiarize the reader with what is arguably the most fundamental philosophical issue by marking out the extremes of the range of positions which can be taken on the essence and goals of the most abstract thought. The hope is that by working through two very different approaches to the issue of the nature of truth and knowledge, the novice will come to understand what a philosophical issue is, as well as the sort of thinking involved in raising and dealing with such an issue. It is further hoped that those more conversant with philosophy will come to appreciate the contemporary challenge to the mainstream by working through the reconception of truth and knowledge and of intellectual inquiry itself.

Part I of the book focuses not on Plato, whose work is too extensive and multi-faceted, but on René Descartes (1596–1650), the first major "modern" philosopher and one who determined the character of subsequent philosophizing about knowledge and truth for some three hundred years. Part II focuses not on Nietzsche, whose work is too enigmatic and diffuse, but on Michel Foucault (1926–84), a contemporary "postmodern" thinker whose views on truth and knowledge were so contrary in content and style that Descartes would not have considered them philosophical. If Descartes was the pre-eminent and archetypal epistemologist, Foucault was the pre-eminent and archetypal antiepistemologist. By contrasting Descartes and Foucault, this book effectively introduces the reader to the currently most important alternative conceptions of truth and knowledge. But perhaps more importantly, by so doing it introduces the reader to the very possibility that there may be alternative conceptions of knowledge and truth, and so of philosophy itself.

With respect to the selection of Descartes and Foucault as the points of contrast, so great is that contrast, and so entrenched are Descartes's views in our present way of thinking, that philosophy students and instructors alike usually think Foucault too difficult a thinker to tackle at an introductory level. Yet these same students and instructors take quite for granted the suitability of Plato or Descartes as subjects of introductory study, in spite of the fact that, unlike Foucault, both propound often perplexing metaphysical theses. The fact is that *any* philosopher of significant stature poses challenges to beginners and experts alike, and what makes Foucault look too difficult has less to do with what he said than with its opposition to and difference from the familiar tradition. What follows will enable access to the subtlety and depth of two philosophers *both* of whose work is as demanding as it has proven productive and influential.

Regarding characterization of basic philosophical stances and the choice of figures for study, Descartes best represents the familiar view that human reason is capable of discerning objective truth, and so of gaining timeless and certain knowledge. Descartes's view was that truth is objective, that it is timeless and autonomous in the sense of being wholly independent of human interests, and that it is accessible to human reason. For Descartes, then, absolute knowledge was possible and was therefore the only proper aim of inquiry. The Cartesian view had Plato as its intellectual progenitor and Immanuel Kant (1724–1804) as its most impressive exponent. ('Cartesian' is the adjectival form of 'Descartes'.) Foucault best represents the antithetical view, which was perhaps most succinctly articulated by Miguel de Cervantes (1547–1616) when he wrote, in *Don Quixote*, that history is the mother of truth. Foucault thought that truth is not objective, that it is made, not found, that it is a product of our interpretive and evaluatory activities rather than something discerned and which we possess when we have knowledge. For Foucault, knowledge is what a given culture deems to be knowledge, what it accepts as authoritative, and clearly that can change with time. This Foucauldian view had G.W.F. Hegel (1770–1831) as its intellectual progenitor and Nietzsche as its most notable exponent. (For easier pronunciation the adjectival form of 'Foucault' is spelled with a 'd' and not the expected 't'.) This latter view holds that what we judge to be true, and hence what we take to be knowledge, is so judged because of broadly historical factors and not in virtue of an intrinsic property. Though it can be traced to Protagoras (481–411 B.C.), this view was most effectively developed in elaboration of Hegel's insight that any claimed truth about ourselves or the world is redescribable in different terms, and so that any claimed knowledge can be shown to be one among various possible construals or interpretations of a given subject. Moreover, on this view, even that something *is* a subject of study and hence possibly a subject of knowledge is itself a function of interpretation. This is a difficult idea that is taken to its limits in the work of Foucault.

As we proceed, contrasting Descartes and Foucault, we will be effectively contrasting the foregoing two conceptions of truth and knowledge. The specific goal is to understand and appreciate the difference between these conceptions as well as what it is for there actually to be alternative conceptions of the nature of knowledge, and so also of what so many people take as unproblematic, namely, the nature of truth. If that much is achieved, this book will have provided considerably more than standard introductions usually succeed in conveying to beginners in philosophy. (See the Bibliography for details on all titles or authors mentioned and all references. References are given as author, date of publication of the edition used, and page or pages.)

DESCARTES AND FOUCAULT

PERHAPS the best way to continue is to say more about the philosophers chosen for contrastive discussion. Descartes's place in the history of philosophy is guaranteed by how his work shaped part of that history. Even Kant, one of history's most difficult and subtle philosophical thinkers, dealt with knowledge mainly in response to the principles established by Descartes, and largely within the methodological tradition Descartes initiated. As for Foucault, the extensive discussion, criticism, and emulation of him in the present and past two decades ensure that his status in future history will be of an order similar to Descartes's. But the importance of these two thinkers is only part of what makes them good choices for discussion and comparison in this text. The other part is the nature of the contrast these two figures provide. Both were immensely influential, but while Descartes defined a core area of philosophy—epistemology—and initiated centuries of effort to ground human knowledge on absolute foundations, Foucault's critiques and positive proposals directly challenged that effort and made it impossible for contemporary and future philosophers to straightforwardly continue Descartes's work or embark on Cartesian projects. The opposition between Descartes and Foucault therefore is not merely one between contrary approaches to an otherwise unproblematic subject matter. The opposition is one between mutually exclusive conceptions of nothing less than philosophy itself.

The reasons why the two highly innovative philosophers considered here were so opposed in their thought are numerous and complex, but one common historical feature does stand out: upheaval in their respective intellectual contexts. In Descartes's time, established assumptions and methods of inquiry were being challenged by exciting new ideas and perspectives on old problems, and by growing impatience with authoritarian intellectual traditions. There was a new confidence and optimism regarding our ability to reason about the world, and a related nascent reliance on experimentation and rigorous theorizing. Most notably, Galileo Galilei (1564–1642) revitalized the till then largely theoretic heliocentrism of Copernicus (1473–1543) with the support of empirical evidence made available by the invention of the telescope. Galileo prompted theological authorities to protest against his work in ways which only underscored the scope and importance of his and others' challenges to then-current intellectual orthodoxy.

In Foucault's time the challenges to established assumptions and modes of inquiry were posed not by success but by failure. In the late 1960s the failure of academic philosophy to show significant progress and result in substantial benefits to intellectual and moral life became evident even to the popular media, and began to assume the proportions of a scandal when some philosophers tried to justify the arcane technicality of their work by describing practical issues as irrelevant to their interests. (Gilbert Ryle once outraged many by answering a newsperson's question as to what he and his colleagues thought about a recent military invasion with: "We're philosophers, not lifeboat men.") The failure of Marxism as a practically realizable ideology was becoming evident to many European intellectuals about the same time, well before the political changes which occurred in Eastern Europe in 1989 and 1990. Additionally, in North America, individualist liberalism was being seen more and more as a political system proving inadequate for dealing with the social problems of the late twentieth century.

The upheaval in their respective times had very different effects on Descartes and Foucault. The main influence on Descartes was a new reliance on the power of reason; the main influence on Foucault was disillusionment with reason as conceived by the Enlightenment. Descartes saw his intellectual predecessors and contemporaries as burdened with dogmatism; Foucault saw his intellectual predecessors and contemporaries as hobbled by precisely the methods and objectives which Descartes thought would ensure intellectual progress. For Descartes, events seemed to confirm the productive power of human reason once it was freed from distorting influences through methodological rigor; for Foucault events seemed to confirm that reason never had been and never could be free of ideology and self-interest.

These generalizations are very broad, but they do suggest how the opposition between Descartes and Foucault is mainly a contrast between intellectual optimism and pessimism about the power of human reason. Perhaps a more accurate characterization is of Descartes as too innocent of the conditioning of reason, and of Foucault as too sophisticated about how reasoning is shaped and directed. In either case, the picture is one of Descartes as a thinker enthusiastic about the potential of human reason as a newly objectified means to cumulative progress in inquiry, and of Foucault as a thinker weary of revelations of how reason is covertly made to serve arational and even irrational ends.

It is worth noting that both figures on whom this book concentrates were French and male. In our time this fact can no longer be taken as it would have been previously, as a matter of course; it now calls for comment. Two explanatory points need to be made, then, about this fact.

The first point will contribute to understanding the foregoing contrast as well as helping explain the choice of Descartes and Foucault as our focal figures. It is a defensible generalization that French thought has been innovative in philosophy more often than it has been developmental. A comparison between Descartes and Kant, as representative French and German thinkers, illustrates the point. Kant's work is considered by most philosophers and historians as deeper and more important than that of Descartes, but Kant's philosophical synthesis, though monumental in conception and implications, was mainly a reaction against the epistemological impasse produced by British and Continental reactions to Descartes's work.

The British reaction to Descartes's work was the empiricism of John Locke (1632–1704), George Berkeley (1685–1753) and David Hume (1711–76). Contrary to Descartes's claim that reason is itself a source of knowledge and not just of instrumental value, the empiricists argued that experience is the sole source of knowledge and reason only the means for productive manipulation of experiential knowledge. These philosophers, especially Hume, were themselves innovative thinkers, but they addressed issues that had been defined by Descartes, and they worked in a polemical environment that owed more of its character, topics and limits to Descartes than to anyone else. And largely for that reason, the empiricists failed to resolve the issues about knowledge which Descartes posed and to which they were reacting, a failure most apparent in the Humean skepticism which prompted Kant's synthesizing efforts.

In discussing Descartes, it will sometimes be necessary to compare or contrast his views with those of Locke and particularly Hume, even if only by implication. The relations between Descartes and Locke and especially Hume are difficult to sketch briefly, but they are important enough to need mention. Aside from the above remarks about empiricism, and what is to be found in the Glossary, perhaps the most crucial point is that Hume's empiricist skepticism was far more thoroughgoing and rigorous than Descartes's philosophical doubt. Hume's, and to a point Locke's, rejection of the *a priori*, of what supposedly could be known as certain on the basis of reason alone—in other words, their rejection of reason itself as a source of substantive knowledge—effectively ended projects such as that of the *Meditations*. Those projects, which began with skepticism about anything not self-evidently true, could not proceed without reason as a distinct source of knowledge and as capable of generating its own criteria for correctness. As we proceed through the discussion of Descartes's project in Part I, it should be increasingly appreciated how much Descartes relies on the *a priori*—and, incidentally, how much he assumes and presupposes in spite of his claims to trust nothing which is not self-evident or derived from rigorous argument.

The Continental response to Descartes was the rationalism of Benedict (Baruch) Spinoza (1632–77) and G. W. Leibniz (1646–1716). Leibniz and Spinoza were also original thinkers, but again they addressed largely the same issues about knowledge and worked in the same polemical environment. Their rationalism—the view that reason is not just instrumental but is itself a source of knowledge—also failed to resolve Descartes's problems and culminated not in skepticism but rather in unworkably complex and hopelessly abstract metaphysical systems. And it is this metaphysical bent which makes the work of Descartes's close rationalist successors less significant for us, since our focus here is epistemology in its purest form.

Locke, Berkeley, Hume, Spinoza, Leibniz and Kant, representing Britain, Holland and Germany, all took their cue from a French innovator. And if we look to the recent past, we find evidence of French intellectual innovation in the organic philosophizing of Henri Bergson (1859–1941); we find it in the semiotics and structuralism of Ferdinand de Saussure (1857–1913), and in their productive development by the literary critic Roland Barthes (1915–80) and the anthropologist Claude Lévi-Strauss (1908–); and we find it in the existentialism of Jean-Paul Sartre (1905–80) which shaped and defined much of European philosophy, literature, and drama for decades. In the 1970s, we find still more evidence of French innovation in the stimulating new ways of philosophizing which Foucault and Jacques Derrida (1930–) had been developing and which began to emerge as France's new contribution to intellectual life. Repudiating structuralism and some of their own earlier work, and indifferent to the Anglo-American philosophical analysis which was coming to be more and more thought of as sterile, Foucault and Derrida initiated the quintessentially postmodern projects of Foucauldian "genealogy" and Derridean "deconstruction": Foucault's meticulous and upending redescriptions of thematic histories, and Derrida's playful unearthing of wholly antithetical elements at the heart of any given position. Not only did these projects enable new ways of philosophizing, they also posed the greatest challenge ever to philosophical reasoning's claimed objectivity and so to claimed philosophical knowledge. Foucault and Derrida extended the "relativistic" theorizing and criticism dominant in the social sciences and literature to philosophy. Up to that time, most professional philosophers had seen relativism as safely contained by the heavily contextual nature of the social sciences and by the supposed irrelevance to their discipline of literature. It was devastating to those same philosophers, therefore, to find their own principles and methods described as contextual and interpretive. The result was that French innovation again prompted productive, if largely defensive, work by philosophers outside France.

The first point about the selection of two French philosophers as the focal figures for this introduction to philosophy, then, is that, given historical precedents, it is no surprise that we find the innovative counterpoint to Descartes's seventeenth century views in late twentieth century French philosophical thought. And of the French philosophers most active in our time, Foucault is the postmodern who has been most widely followed and discussed. Derrida's impact, at least in North America, has been huge in the literary area, but Foucault has been taken up by philosophers, social scientists and others as well as by literary critics. Moreover, because of his work on power-relations, he has also been taken up by many outside the academy, notably policy makers and those who must deal with the architectures of institutions. But perhaps most important is that, at least as far as philosophy is concerned, while Derrida can be emulated, Foucault's work can be *used* in at least some aspects of more traditional projects, and this is attested to by the fact that his views on power-relations are seriously debated by some mainstream philosophers. (Hoy, 1986)

The second point that needs to be made about the choice of Descartes and Foucault, and the one that more directly prompts these explanatory comments, is that because of recent feminist critiques focused on the male-oriented and Eurocentric character of traditional philosophy, it is necessary explicitly to acknowledge and justify the selection of Foucault, another European male, as the most suitable counterpoint to Descartes. That Descartes was male needs no comment beyond noting that no female philosophers succeeded in having the same influence and achieving the same importance in the seventeenth century. And while perhaps problematic, that Descartes and Foucault were both Europeans is, for our present purposes, unavoidable, since the objective is to understand traditional epistemology-oriented philosophy and its most imposing and immediate alternative. But contemporary feminist critiques of "patriarchal" philosophizing are as much repudiations of Descartes's views as is Foucault's work. So it seems a feminist epistemologist is potentially as suitable a counterpoint to Descartes as is Foucault, and that choosing Foucault over one of them could be to display a sexist bias.

The difficulty is that feminist epistemology is still largely embryonic, and feminist epistemological critiques are presently diverse in focus, content, and approach. At the present time there is no one such critique that is both widely enough accepted and adequately enough developed to successfully challenge Foucault's work as the most suitable counterpoint to Descartes's epistemology. Moreover, choosing a particular text to contrast with Descartes's *Meditations on First Philosophy* poses serious problems at this juncture, not only because of diversity of content, but because of the lack of adequate consensus on what constitutes a properly feminist work. For example, I considered Lorraine Code's *Epistemic Respon-*

sibility as an appropriate work because of its cohesive and strongly anti-Cartesian content, but it was not thought to be sufficiently feminist in character by feminists I consulted. On the other hand, books such as Evelyn Fox Keller's *Gender and Science* and Sandra Harding and Merrill Hintikka's *Discovering Reality*, though accepted as adequately feminist, in being collections of articles mainly critical of present conceptions of science and epistemology, are rather too focused and do not present a sufficiently cohesive positive position to serve as an adequate contrast to Descartes's highly unified but still very general views. In any case, Foucault is not as distant from feminism as his gender might suggest. While Foucault was not a feminist, much of what he had to say about power-relations is highly relevant to feminism, and much of Foucault's critique of traditional philosophy not only is compatible with many feminist critiques, but augments and supports some of those critiques. Additionally, Foucault's antiessentialism is a feature common to both his and most feminist positions. However, Foucault's relation to feminism is a complex issue on which there is a broad diversity of views which we cannot pursue here. (Diamond and Quinby, 1988)

Aside from ensuring that this book treats two philosophers of appropriate stature, the selection of Descartes and Foucault as objects of study provides an extremely productive intellectual contrast. Not only will this contrast allow appreciation of the range of positions available with respect to theorizing about truth and knowledge, it is a contrast which captures what many see as philosophy's worst crisis to date. Descartes worked to insure that philosophical inquiry would have a bright, fruitful and limitless future. But Foucault in particular and postmoderns in general offer a future in which the sort of inquiry Descartes envisioned and tried to conduct is regarded as at best naive and at worst self-deceived. Where Descartes sought to arrive at truth by the exercise of pure reason guided by rigorous methodology, Foucault provided destructive combinations of genealogical analyses and persuasive redescriptions. That is, Foucault showed, particularly in his work after 1968, how notions we take as unquestionable or "natural" come to be so taken, and he did so by retelling the histories of those notions, by focusing on the marginal and ignored, the suppressed and supposedly irrelevant. In this way Foucault developed histories with different emphases and priorities, histories which by their difference throw into sharp relief the contingency of generally accepted ones. In *The History of Sexuality*, for instance, Foucault traced the neglected aspects of the history of how we came to construe sex as we do, to show that rather than being the subject of repression since the Victorian era, sex is treated and discussed with obsessive persistence. This is how Foucault effectively redescribed how some traditional interpretations and construals arose and developed, and how their most central ideas originated. His redescriptive narrations showed further how those central ideas then ossified into articles of faith, and how their touted objectivity was actually only a favored perspective. Foucault's narrational reconstructions of position-defining sets of integrated assumptions, methods, claimed truths and supposed knowledge reveal how those positions are only so many proposed construals of their subject-matters, rather than being elaborations of discerned and articulated actualities.

Given diffuse but surprisingly tenacious expectations, it may not be altogether clear how the foregoing sort of exercise relates to philosophy, since it may sound like more properly the doing of history or social science. However, the point is that the very existence of Foucault's reconstructive narratives about the nature and history of diverse institutions like the clinic, the prison and the asylum, and more abstract institutions like human sexuality, impugned not only specific traditional conceptions and accounts of those institutions, but also the underlying reasoned inquiry which supposedly established those traditional conceptions and accounts through what is presented as rigorous investigation and analysis. In short, the mere availability of Foucault's plausible reconstruals meant that accepted accounts of the institutions considered had no inviolate status since, to the extent that Foucault was successful, those accounts were shown to have viable alternatives. And if accepted accounts were shown not to be the only possible accounts of the institutions in question, they then could not be the inevitable results of successful truth-seeking inquiry. Foucault's work cast doubt on the very idea of a correct account precisely by providing alternative accounts, and it therefore casts doubt on the methods by which correct accounts are allegedly discovered. The result is that professional philosophers who endorse Cartesian principles are currently faced with a hard choice between dogmatically retaining those principles in spite of Foucault's and similar challenges, or producing new ones which preserve the essential commitment to objective truth and truth-discerning methods of inquiry, but which are not vulnerable to the acid-bath of Foucauldian redescription.

How better to be introduced to philosophy, then, than to be initiated into the most portentous contemporary philosophical debate. And since the Cartesian side of that debate represents the epistemological core of traditional philosophy, by coming to understand the debate the novice will learn the gist of what more orthodox introductory texts attempt to teach and which they usually present as the whole of philosophy. In addition the novice will learn about the conceptual options that make our time one of exciting intellectual change and opportunity. As for more knowledgeable readers, what follows will enable them to appreciate how and why that about which they are knowledgeable has been impugned by the work of some of its inheritors.

HOW TO USE THIS BOOK

THE guiding principle of this book's preparation was that an introduction to philosophy should not try to cover great stretches of philosophical territory with inevitably inadequate and often confusing exposition. Instead, a better introduction to philosophy might be an effective and engaging presentation of a sharp contrast of perspectives on one or other of philosophy's most representative and basic issues. Rather than offer a mass of data, an introduction to philosophy should immediately engage the reader in an important ongoing debate which demonstrates the nature of philosophy, presents a crucially consequential issue, and captures the imagination. This book does not try to give an outline of the discipline which, while informative, would be too abstract and overly extensive to prompt and support real interest. Nor does it attempt the impossible task of adequately covering even the major aspects of philosophy in sufficient depth to guarantee productive engagement. Instead, the whole idea is to present an interesting and accessible clash of views that will illustrate what characterizes serious philosophizing. The hope is that once it is understood what Descartes tried to do, and how and why Foucault tried to undo Descartes's claimed achievements, the reading of other philosophers in a reasonably sophisticated and informed way will be possible. Philosophy is not a subject to be learned in the sense of adding to one's store of information; it is a way of thinking, and it is best learned through detailed discussion of two sides of a reasonably manageable issue rather than through extensive survey.

The present book is perhaps best described as an extended discussion designed to complement Descartes's *Meditations on First Philosophy* and Foucault's *The History of Sexuality, Volume I: An Introduction*. ("The History of Sexuality" applies to three completed volumes of a projected six volumes. See Foucault, 1980b:187. Volume One, originally *The Will to Know*, is titled *The History of Sexuality* in English. Volumes Two and Three are *The Use of Pleasure* and *The Care of the Self*.) What this book says about Descartes and Foucault relates immediately to these most central of their works, and while this book is self-contained, what it attempts to achieve will not be achieved unless those works are read. This book includes some quoted passages from the works considered, but the works must be read carefully and in their entirety for full appreciation of what is here provided. Nor is that a daunting prospect, for unlike most philosophical books, both are very short. The *Meditations* is a booklet of some eighty-five pages, and while *The History of Sexuality* is about twice as long, it is still brief and is captivatingly written. As to how one might best proceed, with respect to reading this and the other two books, there are three options: to read this book first, or to read it along with the *Meditations* and/or *The History of Sexuality*, or to read the latter books first. In my estimation these options are in proper order of preference. I think it would be most productive to read this book first, and somewhat less so to try to read this book and one or both of the others concurrently. And I think that to read the *Meditations* or *The History of Sexuality* first might well result in the formation of counterproductive impressions which could hinder progress. I shall proceed, then, on the assumption that this book will be read first, and present my remarks and the various quotations in line with that assumption.

At this point it may be useful to caution the novice against possible initial frustration. The special presentation of philosophy in this book will probably not be wholly clear until most of the book has been read and at least substantial parts of the *Meditations* and *The History of Sexuality* have been read. And this is due not to some perversity of presentation, but to the very nature of philosophizing. Most people interested in learning philosophy think that doing so is a matter of learning *about* philosophy, as is the case with most subjects such as history or geology. They expect, then, that their progress will be steady and incremental, and they are not prepared to feel lost except at the very beginning of their study. That expectation, and the impatience it fosters, are detrimental to the study and understanding of philosophy. "Philosophy" is less the name of a unitary discipline or cohesive body of knowledge than of a way of thinking and looking at things: a way of thinking that allows tremendous variation with respect to content and methodology. What makes being introduced to philosophy particularly difficult is that learning about philosophy requires learning how to *do* philosophy. If one wants to learn philosophy, one must learn how to think philosophically. And until philosophical thinking is learned, at least to some degree, there will be inadequate appreciation of the nature of philosophy. There is a sense, then, in which the reader should not expect to fully appreciate what is in this book, and in the related texts, until all three have been read. And this does not apply only to the novice. Those familiar with mainstream philosophical issues and methods will need to work through this book and Foucault's text before appreciating the challenge Foucault poses to the Cartesian legacy. What is interesting is that for novice or expert, the very contrast I am concerned to draw will reveal that the things Descartes and Foucault were doing are of a kind, in spite of great differences in conception, methodology, objectives, and detail; the contrast will itself reveal that both Descartes and Foucault were philosophizing.

The significance of the affirmation that Descartes and Foucault both did philosophy, in spite of the radical differences to be discussed below, is that philosophy is a manner of thought which claims a 2,500-year recorded history, and which for most of that time has been construed as the uniquely rational way to deal with the deepest and most complex questions we have asked. Now, as at few times in the past, practitioners of this discipline are divided as to the nature, status, and prospects of what they do. Some hold to the traditional conception; others think the traditional conception is radically flawed. For the first group, philosophy goes on as before, though once again challenged. For the second group, philosophy cannot continue as before. But not even the most radical (Rorty, 1982) think philosophy, as highly abstract thought, should be *abandoned*—assuming we could do so. The question is how to continue it. To understand this question, someone new to philosophy must learn both the traditional conception and the contemporary alternative; and someone familiar with traditional philosophy must learn the nature of the contemporary alternative's challenge. However, to systematically familiarize oneself with the full spectrum of philosophical issues from both the traditional and currently critical perspectives would be a formidable undertaking for both those unfamiliar with philosophy and those familiar with only its more traditional side. As suggested, therefore, the more productive way to proceed is to focus on the major and most contrary positions on a fundamental aspect of philosophizing. In what follows we will do just that, by considering how issues about knowledge and truth are treated by two philosophers who represent opposite extremes on the possibility of epistemology, and so on the possibility of traditional philosophy. Familiarizing oneself with these two thinkers will enable better understanding of the traditional philosophical search for truth, as well as enabling appreciation of how that search can be critically redescribed as only the product of a special history. And it is in the interplay between these two extremes that we find what is most challenging, intriguing and promising in contemporary philosophy.

Having said the foregoing about the book and philosophy generally, a word now about how the book is something of a guerrilla exercise. Conventional introductions to philosophy often devote a surprisingly small proportion of space to epistemology, usually treating it as one topic among several. But epistemology or the theory of knowledge is fundamental to traditional philosophy. The heart of Platonic/Cartesian/Kantian philosophy is that epistemological inquiry can lead to the achievement of knowledge about reason, truth, and knowledge themselves. To raise the issue about the viability of epistemology, then, is to raise the issue of whether philosophizing can be a means to knowledge more fundamental than any other. And in considering this issue, this book runs counter to more orthodox introductions to philosophy generally and to epistemology in particular by actually being an introduction to questions more basic than any which those more orthodox introductory texts cover. That is why, even if it turns out that, apparent history notwithstanding, traditional epistemology is only a long-lived confusion, and all of traditional philosophy falls with it, this book would not be an introduction to a nonexistent subject. The reason is that, in investigating the very possibility of traditional philosophy, we are philosophizing.

We philosophize whenever we try to understand how things "hang together" in the most general way, and that is to follow in the spirit of Socrates (469–399 B.C.) and Kant, if not precisely in their footsteps. We may have to abandon a number of traditional methods and assumptions, perhaps even the current conception of the entire discipline, but that does not mean we cannot continue to think critically and in a holistic way about the broadest issues that concern us. Nor would the abandonment of absolutes mean that henceforth no judgment we might make could be justified. Rejection of one manner of justification, regardless of how well established and apparently sacrosanct, is not necessarily rejection of the possibility of showing judgments to be warranted. The contemporary challenge that Foucault poses for the traditional philosopher is exactly how to show judgments to be warranted without appealing to metaphysical grounds or a Cartesian God whose reason for existing is no more than to underwrite what we believe and value. Consideration of Foucault's challenge to philosophy is interestingly and even paradoxically an exercise that, if seriously pursued, leaves no option but the doing of philosophy. As Foucault himself tells us,

> Western philosophy, since Descartes . . . has always been involved with the problem of knowledge. If someone wanted to be a philosopher but didn't ask . . . 'What is knowledge?' or 'What is truth?' [how] could one say he was a philosopher? And for all that I may like to say that I am not a philosopher, nonetheless if my concern is with truth then I am still a philosopher. (Foucault, 1980b:66)

SOME PRACTICAL CONSIDERATIONS

W<small>HETHER</small> or not philosophy is new to the reader, there is good advice available on how to read philosophical works: a work in philosophy, basic or advanced, should first be read once through without too much concern with what may be initially obscure or complex. The point is to get a rough idea of the sort of work it is, of what is emphasized and reiterated, and what large claims are made and conclusions drawn. The entire work, or at least a substantial part of it, should then be re-read. But this time it should be read much more slowly and thoughtfully. It is very surprising how simple repetition will clarify difficult passages. This text, the *Meditations*, and *The History of Sexuality* are all brief works. The first was written, and the other two selected, precisely to facilitate and encourage repeated reading.

The next step is to read the material again, whether it has been read two or even three times. But now it should be read in what is best described as a wary way. That is, one should be looking for things that seem at odds with other parts of the text, for ideas that emerge but are not argued for or made explicit, for complex discussions that leave the reader perplexed or appear to come to little. The material should now be read probingly; the reader should look beneath the surface by asking such questions as: What does someone have to believe or be thinking to say just this? and, Why should someone think that to be obvious? There is also a need to be alert for ordinary words being used in special ways, such as when Descartes talks about thoughts as "ideas," thereby effectively assimilating sensation to reflection. The author may be trying to win acceptance of something by trading on the ordinary sense of a word while using it in a special way. This is an important point and merits somewhat fuller discussion here, even though we are still concerned with preliminaries.

Much of the time when Descartes is talking about "ideas," and seems to be talking about what is familiar enough to us, what he is really concerned with is a particular conception of the nature of our awareness. The conception in question is of awareness as consciousness of "internal" representations of objects "external" to the mind. In this way, by talking easily about the contents of awareness as so many ideas, Descartes may succeed in winning acceptance of the notion that our awareness of the world is a matter of having mental copies in our minds of the things that make up the world. By introducing this problematic internal/external distinction with respect to our awareness and the objects of our awareness, Descartes surreptitiously but effectively reconceives the nature of awareness by his special use of the terms 'idea' and 'ideas' and succeeds in isolating us in our own minds. Then he can generate the problem of how we ever manage to gain knowledge about what is "outside" our minds. Moreover, when one reads Descartes's definition of 'ideas' as comprising all that we are aware of, it is crucial to realize that he is in effect reducing complex sensations and emotions to ideas entertained by a mind which begins to seem more and more detached from its contents. But more on this later. The point here is that reading philosophy is difficult, and it must be read repeatedly, carefully, thoroughly and warily for the reader to gain full understanding of what is going on.

There are a number of other points to make regarding how philosophy should be read. One must be alert for inconsistencies, and not only inconsistencies of a large sort, as when fairly major claims conflict with one another. It is also important to look out for ambiguities in key terms, ambiguities which may mask real tensions in the author's thought. Another key to effective reading of philosophy is being alert to lack of contrast: when something is claimed in a work, it must be considered whether there is a significant alternative. Some philosophical claims are so hedged or so general that they are actually compatible with just about anything. There is need to be mindful of possible counterexamples, of what would conflict with what is being claimed. If nothing would, then nothing significant is being claimed.

Still another thing to keep in mind when reading philosophy
has to do with criteria for correctness. When claims are made, ask
yourself how one would go about finding out or deciding if those
claims are warranted or not. In most of what we encounter outside
philosophy this question is usually answerable in empirical terms:
that is, we can check to see if some state of affairs is or is not the
case. But when something is problematic in philosophy, we cannot
just go and look; we cannot settle issues by observation of or experimentation with overtly accessible situations. Some philosophical
claims are supported by specific arguments, but many are based
on appeals to reason. And even where an argument is provided,
there is always room to question the premises or the interpretations
it presupposes. Therefore, one has to ask what sorts of things could
possibly be done to support or undermine a philosophical claim.
For instance, philosophers often use "thought experiments" or
carefully described imaginary situations to support or impugn their
claims. The object of such experiments is to test—and supposedly
make clear—the acceptability of some description or contention.
The point is to illustrate complex situations in which we do not
know what to say about something, with imagined simpler situations
where things can be made much clearer and our inclinations more
evident. The underlying assumption is that so long as we are careful
to be "objective," those inclinations will afford reliable guidelines,
since they are taken as rooted in our rationality. However, in using
devices like thought experiments, we may only be favoring problematic intuitions which are products of our training and expectations, rather than truths demonstrated by our rationality. It is
crucially important, then, to think hard about what criteria are
employed to judge a philosophical contention or conclusion correct
or incorrect.

To conclude this consideration of practical or methodological
matters, it should be noted that something people invariably forget
or perversely ignore when they read philosophy is common sense.
Because philosophy is thought to be esoteric and difficult, people
often read it in an overly forgiving or credulous way, and this is
by no means the case only among novices. Sophistication in philosophy can sometimes prompt too great a tolerance, if not cre-
dulity, with respect to what appears highly complex and convoluted
and is then judged to be deep and important. In fact, one sometimes
feels that when people read philosophy they expect and even want
obscurity. But philosophers are as capable of being wrong or unclear as anyone else, and depth or correctness should not be as-

sumed on the basis of the difficulty or unfamiliarity of what is read. Readers must not be afraid to consider that something is confused or wrongheaded. The other side of this is that just because something is not readily understood, it is not necessarily wrong or confused. Nor should there be unreasonable resistance to what is initially strange. A philosophical work must be read in as open-minded and flexible a way as possible. After all, philosophers are concerned to change their readers' thinking at the most fundamental level, and if one is to benefit from what they say, there is need to allow the deepest assumptions and values to be challenged. A difficult balance must be struck, then, between being gullible and being open minded. Consider two of the claims to be encountered in what follows: Descartes will contend that at this precise moment you may be dreaming, and Foucault will contend that rather than Victorian culture suppressing sexuality, it facilitated an obsessive interest in sex by developing discourses and practices which presented sex as a proper object of theory and investigation. In the first case, there may be a strong inclination to dismiss something that appears absurd; in the second case, a novel perspective may appear intriguing. But it must be seriously considered whether the first claim is possibly also a worthwhile novel perspective, and initial reactions must be examined for signs of intellectual complacency. Additionally, a ready interest in the second claim must be subjected to careful scrutiny to determine if it is prompted more by predispositions than by real merit.

All of this may seem initially overwhelming, but I can promise that after sufficient reading it will be easier. But having said a little about our focal figures, the nature of the opposition between them, and about the book itself, it will prove useful to now provide a context for consideration of the views of Descartes and Foucault.

THE CONTEXT

T HE FIRST of the two main parts of this book begins with consideration of the epistemological views of Descartes, the so-called "Father of Modern Philosophy." This title does not attribute to Descartes merely the invention and initiation of a more up-to-date way of philosophizing than that of the Ancients and Medievals he followed. The term 'modern' in philosophy and intellectual history has a deeper meaning. This meaning has to do with the conception and place of reason in the project of aspired-to subjugation of all aspects of nature to human understanding and control. Descartes fathered modern philosophy by reconceiving philosophical activity. He turned his back on philosophy as metaphysical and ethical speculation heavily influenced and constrained by theology. Up to his time philosophy had been an enterprise mostly concerned with elaborating the postulated, and usually theologically dictated, nature of "ultimate" reality, deriving rules for human conduct from an equally postulated human nature, and attempting to rationally justify religious claims. But of greater relevance here is that Descartes shifted philosophical interest from *being* to *knowing*, from considerations of what exists and the nature of the existent, to investigation of how we know and what we can know. Charles Sanders Peirce (1839–1914) nicely summarizes "the spirit of Cartesianism" by saying that it taught that "philosophy must begin with universal doubt," and that "the ultimate test of certainty is to be found in the individual consciousness." (Buchler, 1955:228) Supposedly, philosophy, and by extension all inquiry, begins with skepticism, with the demand that what appears to be the case be demonstrated by reason to actually *be* the case. And the ultimate test of what is the case is what is given to consciousness in an undoubtable way. It is this egocentric skepticism which perhaps most crucially characterizes modern philosophy. (Note that the terms 'egocentric' and 'egoistic' in philosophy have to do with what focuses on the ego or the self as an entity, and that they differ from the pejoratives 'self-centered' and 'egotistic'.) The centrality of this skepticism is evident in the fact that it is just this egocentric skepticism that is rejected even by less-than-radical contemporary critics of modern thinking. For example, Hans-Georg Gadamer, though in the same broad "Continental" tradition as Foucault, and also a critic of modern or Cartesian thinking, does not approach the radicalness of Foucault. Nonetheless, in his "Hermeneutics as Practical Philosophy," Gadamer rejects egocentric skepticism by rejecting its obverse, namely, the view that Peirce describes as conviction that the ultimate test of certainty is to be found in the individual consciousness. Gadamer argues that Nietzsche rightly demanded that we "doubt more profoundly and fundamentally than . . . Descartes . . . [by] calling into doubt . . . the testimony of human reflective consciousness." (Baynes, 1987:330)

Convinced of the need to begin with general skepticism, Descartes proposed making philosophy into a scientific project for the discovery of truth. His major innovative proposal was to pursue what he conceived of as certain knowledge by employing a supposedly rigorous, foolproof, and unique methodology for arriving at truth. And the advance he made on the discursive investigatory method which Plato called "dialectic," and which was offered as just such a way to achieve truth, was that Descartes followed Galileo in aspiring to geometric practice and rigor and proposed that inquiry should be *analytic*. This meant that inquiry should be a search for truth by the breaking-down into basic components of anything we find problematic. Descartes argued that by identifying and getting clear on the most basic elements of mental and physical reality, we could then go on to learn all that those elements could comprise; in other words, all there is to know.

It is notable that Descartes's methodological proposals should be fairly easy to grasp even for the novice, because they are deeply embedded in our still largely modern way of thinking. More difficult to understand are Descartes's philosophical assumptions and maneuvers, some of which are little more than leaps of faith, regardless of his protestations. But by the end of Part I, the reader should have a firm grip on traditional epistemology-based philosophy and be prepared to consider Foucault's challenge to it.

To proceed, we must return to Plato and Aristotle (384–322 B.C.) with whom it all really began—always allowing for seminal contributions by Socrates and some of the pre-Socratics. Plato initiated epistemology by arguing that real knowledge was only possible of objects that were eternal and unchanging. Anything less than knowing how things are eternally, how they must always be, would be uncertain and vulnerable to change, to amendment, to revision, and so not really be knowledge. He thought mathematics to be the paradigm of knowledge, conceiving of mathematics as the objective study of real and eternal entities as opposed to being the development of formal systems relating abstractions in defined ways. Plato so distrusted the changing world that he thought we could not really know anything about it. He believed we could only form opinions regarding what was inherently unknowable because intrinsically unstable. Once this way of thinking was introduced, it became inevitable that many would concern themselves with testing putative knowledge to see if it met the Platonic standard, and that they would try to ground "opinion" about the world on more reliable knowledge, which is precisely to do traditional epistemology.

Aristotle was rather more practically inclined than his teacher, Plato, and pursued every avenue of inquiry open to him, but notably warned us about not seeking more precision in inquiry than a subject allows. Aristotle said that we all "by nature . . . desire to know." (Kiernan, 1962:315) He believed that human nature is such that we want to learn as much as we can about ourselves and the world. Today we find his view, that some primordial human nature dictates our interests and behavior, very problematic. But history shows that we must in any case modify Aristotle's claim, for history has followed Plato more than Aristotle. At least the history of philosophy is better described as a record of human efforts not only to gain knowledge, but to achieve certainty about ourselves and the world in which we find ourselves. Rather than a curiosity-driven project of open inquiry, our intellectual history has been a quest for absolutes. For most participants in that history, knowing has been and is knowing with certainty, or it is not knowing at all. This epistemic intransigence has had more to do with determining the nature of philosophizing than any natural curiosity we may be heirs to.

Something else Aristotle said was that a true proposition or statement is one which "asserts that what is, is." (Kiernan, 1962:496) Achieving knowledge, then, must be the discernment of truth, for to have knowledge is to be able to formulate statements which say how things are, and only if we discover how things are do we achieve knowledge. But while Aristotle may have tolerated varying degrees of knowledge, Descartes, who directly influenced modern epistemology far more than Plato or Aristotle, unfortunately followed Plato's lead regarding knowledge. For him truth was how things are absolutely, and to discern truth is to discover how things are and must be. Like Plato, Descartes thought that to be knowledge something had to be known with absolute certainty. What he shared with Plato was the idea that there is objective truth to be discerned, and that we have ways of discerning it. There is no concession made here to the degree of precision a subject matter admits; the expectation is that the subject matter of real knowledge must always be determinate and absolute.

Against Plato and Descartes, Foucault thought that the very notions of objective truth and certain knowledge are misconceived. Foucault did not think philosophizing was a way of even approaching such truth and knowledge. He did not think that Plato's and Descartes's projects were possible. Instead he thought that rather than Plato and Descartes having launched a worthwhile quest for truth, much less having discerned important truths about reality and the nature of knowledge, what they actually did was initiate and develop a way of thinking that has persisted for centuries as a particular construal of ourselves, our capacities, and the world. The irony is that Plato and Descartes were successful enough that many take their view as not a construal at all, but as the objective reality of human knowledge and inquiry.

The opposition between Descartes's view of us as inquirers discovering objective truth, and Foucault's view of us as participants in truth-determining practices, might look like one between philosophy and its utter negation. But as suggested in the last section, this is not the case. While philosophy in any given age is identified with how it is done in that age, the term 'philosophy' denotes a kind and level of very abstract thought and inquiry which may be conducted in numerous ways. Foucault certainly did not do philosophy as Descartes or Kant did, and whether or not Foucault did philosophy at all is a question many take seriously. (O'Farrell, 1989) But Foucault did do philosophy in a perfectly straightforward sense. To better understand how this is so, one needs to appreciate Wilfrid Sellars's working definition of philosophy, alluded to above, of philosophizing as thinking, in the most general way, about how things hang together, in the most general way. Foucault certainly did that.

Regardless of how extreme the opposition between Descartes and Foucault, it is actually encompassed by philosophy conceived in Sellars's way as inquiry at the broadest and most abstract level. The fairly continuous certainty-oriented epistemological tradition encompassing Plato, Descartes, Kant, and many contemporaries may define philosophy for most people. But the fact that that tradition excludes and is repudiated by Foucault and others of like mind does not mean that they are not philosophers. It is precisely a postmodernist contention that there simply is no single thing that is philosophy properly done; that intellectual inquiry at the highest levels can take very diverse forms and employ equally diverse methods and criteria.

For most, 'philosophy' usually conjures up issues about ethics, freedom of the will, the nature of the soul, God and "ultimate reality." Many people turn to philosophy to resolve moral problems; to get clear about their freedom and responsibilities as agents; to fathom their nature as living, aware beings; to understand their religious legacies or inclinations; and to wonder about the "meaning" of existence. But all of these projects, which are often ill-conceived, begin with several traditional assumptions: that philosophy can succeed as a method, that its criteria for correctness work, that abstract truths are attainable by the use of rational methods, and that conclusions reached through discursive reasoning will be correct independently of any individual's or group's interests. In fact, these assumptions run so deep and are so widespread that most people who turn to philosophy do so precisely because they are convinced that only philosophy provides an avenue to truth about the deep issues that concern them. They believe that only philosophy has the method and the criteria to achieve certainty about fundamental matters. In short, they believe that philosophy as Plato, Descartes and Kant conceived it just is the properly rational way to tackle our deepest questions. These same people, taking traditional philosophy as the only ultimately reliable way of inquiry, are therefore not prepared to question philosophy itself. They are not prepared to wonder about the feasibility of what they see as the highest use of abstract reasoning. We can say of them that they are followers of Plato and Descartes, who think that the philosophical project is at base the reasoned discovery of ultimate truth.

Others, roughly characterizable as Nietzschean in their attitudes, think that the foregoing view of philosophy is little more than wishful thinking and an exercise in communal rationalization of cherished beliefs and values. These others think that the only truth we discover is the truth we make, that the methods and criteria we use are themselves products of our interpretive activities, and that our conceptions of reason and rationality change with our beliefs and values. Philosophy for them, rather than being uniquely correct reasoning at its deepest and most rigorous, is only how we work out our most basic commitments, how we justify our firmest beliefs. Philosophy for them, rather than being thinking at its most general and abstract, is how we define and determine thinking at its most general and abstract.

The basic Platonic/Cartesian view needs little exposition because of its general familiarity and centrality in our culture. And because of that familiarity and centrality, it is the view that seems most natural and least problematic. The person most innocent of philosophy will readily recognize the idea that truth is objective and eternal, as well as the idea that knowledge is the discernment of such truth. But the Nietzschean view is unfamiliar and elusive. How might someone come to think that there is no capital-T Truth to discover, that there are only ways of making small-t truths? How might someone come to believe that knowledge is partly a matter of determination and decision, a matter of what is judged to be knowledge instead of what must be knowledge?

Some people turn to philosophy not because they are moved by ethical or metaphysical questions, but because they are perplexed by knowledge itself. This is particularly likely to happen in times when there are great intellectual changes taking place, as when Descartes tried to ensure that intellectual inquiry would proceed on so solid a basis that it would yield permanently unchangeable results. In spite of the dominance of the Platonic/Cartesian view, in our time psychological and sociological sophistication have made it seem to many that nothing can be true except from a particular perspective, at a particular time, and for a limited number of people or even a single individual. There is, then, ample occasion to wonder about knowledge. Still, most who do question the nature of knowledge find it very difficult to accept what Nietzsche called "perspectivism" and others call relativism. So, like Descartes, they try to establish something as always and forever true in order to have a base on which to ground everything else. For them the postmodern challenge to epistemology calls for more and better epistemology, not its reconception or abandonment. But at least since the nineteenth century, a few of those perplexed by knowledge have been convinced that there is something very wrong about both the felt need for certainty and the belief that it is attainable, and they have tried to understand how our judgments are hemmed in by time and place, by history and expectations.

The first way of philosophizing about truth and knowledge, trying to discern capital-T Truth, is traditional or modern epistemology: it is to engage in intellectual investigation of knowledge itself in order to tell when we actually have knowledge, and so justify or ground what we deem to be knowledge. The second way of proceeding, trying to understand how what we know is a function of who we are and what we do, is in effect a matter of showing that traditional or modern epistemology simply cannot be done. It is to contend that knowledge is forever circumscribed by language and culture, and so that no kind of inquiry, no matter how rigorous, can yield ahistoric certainty. It is to contend that there is no neutral position from which we can investigate knowledge and judge it timelessly sound. It is to contend, then, that knowledge as Descartes conceived it is not only unattainable but is actually not a meaningful idea. It is, finally, to contend that epistemology must be naturalized, which is to say epistemological questions must be shorn of their metaphysical trappings and turned over to psychologists and other scientists to be considered and resolved in the context of empirical theories and data about thinking and learning.

The answer to the question of how someone might come to doubt the Cartesian nature of truth and reason, then, is that once we encounter an alternative to something we have accepted unquestioningly, whether by reading a book that challenges our basic beliefs or by traveling in a different culture, we realize that what we believe or how we do things is just one way of thinking and one way of acting. When we encounter a jarring difference of perspective or practice we may appreciate the point of Nietzsche's remark: "This is my way; where is yours? *the* way . . . does not exist." (Nietzsche, 1968:307) Once this realization occurs our Cartesian certainty in our own beliefs and practices evaporates. Those who come to doubt Cartesian assumptions, therefore, are those who have at least glimpsed alternatives to them and taken those alternatives seriously.

Unfortunately, the realization that there are alternatives to anything we believe firmly does not always occur, regardless of the diversity of thought and behavior encountered. It is perfectly possible never to question what we believe and prize, regardless of opportunity. And if we do not, we are the losers for it. This book is designed to confront the novice with two conceptions of truth and knowledge, a tacitly accepted but likely unexamined one, and another which must initially seem intellectually threatening. The book is also designed to confront the expert and near-expert with what must initially seem an affront to their expertise. The book attempts to accomplish these goals by providing a contrastive encounter with two radically different perspectives on truth and knowledge, and every effort has been made to make those perspectives accessible and compelling. This is, then, an opportunity to reflect critically on your views and assumptions about truth and knowledge. What you do with the opportunity is, of course, up to you.

PART I

DESCARTES

THE STANDARD VIEW

RENÉ DESCARTES is usually pictured as an intellectual revolutionary, as someone concerned to introduce something quite novel to philosophical thinking. This is largely due to the too-ready assimilation of notable thinkers from Galileo to Newton as uniformly enthusiastic disparagers of medieval methods and assumptions. (Debus, 1978) This common view of Descartes and his project is rather dubious in that it at least misconstrues his motivation. Rather than to revolutionize philosophy, what Descartes actually sought to achieve with his admittedly innovative skeptical method was a very conservative objective: to ensure that human knowledge would never again be as radically challenged and disrupted as it had been by his contemporary Galileo. Descartes saw challenge and disruption as possible only because of prior error, so he sought to preclude further intellectual revolution by grounding knowledge in utterly reliable unchanging truths and fundamental first principles. He believed that once we discerned those truths and principles, we could go about the detailed business of developing knowledge with the assurance that our cognitive achievements would stand for all time.

The crucial thing to understand about Descartes is that he thought knowledge, both actual and possible, to be of a piece, to be unitary in a way we now have difficulty understanding, and so to be capable of being grounded on common basic principles. As C. P. Snow (1905–80) has told us, our culture distinguishes sharply between the humanities on the one hand and the sciences on the other. Additionally, it thinks of the sciences and humanities as themselves divided into areas and sub-areas, such as biology and chemistry, literature and history. This fragmentation of knowledge precludes that one discipline or sort of inquiry will be considered directly relevant to another, to say nothing of Descartes's view that they have the same grounds and so are capable of justification in the same way. Descartes would have been baffled by contemporary disciplinary divisions. To him knowledge was whole and totally rational, so it was possible to ground it all on a relatively few truths and principles. And once we had those basics, we could, given enough time and sufficiently careful effort, deduce the whole of the rest of possible knowledge, needing experience only to test, expand, and apply our reasoning. Descartes seems to have genuinely thought that he could articulate for us all we needed to begin an ages-long task of discerning and formulating all that can be known.

The initial and most important item Descartes sought in his enterprise was a single unquestionable truth that would serve as the base for an inverted pyramid of ever more complex knowledge, and that would provide a fundamental and utterly reliable standard to test anything which we thought might be true. Descartes reminds us that "Archimedes . . . demanded nothing more than a fixed and immovable fulcrum," and Descartes assumed he would have his epistemic Archimedean fulcrum if he could "find a single truth which is certain and indubitable." (Descartes, 2:23 [I:149]. Note that references to Descartes's *Meditations* will give the number of the meditation, rather than the less informative edition date, and the page. In a few cases the title of another of Descartes's works will be given as part of a reference. Unless otherwise specified, all references to the *Meditations* are to the Macmillan/Library of Liberal Arts 1951 edition, which is perhaps the most readily available and least expensive, as well as possibly the most used—the 1989 reprint used is the thirty-first printing. To facilitate comparison of translations, volume and page references are given [in square brackets] to the standard edition of Descartes's collected works by Haldane and Ross, 1969.)

Descartes thought that to get the necessary sample of truth he had to subject everything he believed to the most stringent doubt in the hope of finding something which he could not doubt and which would therefore be revealed as absolutely true. He proceeded, then, to "abstain from . . . belief in things which are not entirely certain and indubitable no less . . . than from . . . belief in those which appear to me to be manifestly false. . . ." (Descartes, 1:17. Here Haldane and Ross offer a perhaps clearer rendition and have Descartes being "no less careful to withhold . . . assent from matters which are not entirely certain and indubitable than from those which [actually] appear . . . false." [I:145]) In short, Descartes set out to dismiss as false anything which was open to the slightest doubt. His point of departure was that discovery of truth could only be as sound as the thoroughness of his methodological skepticism.

The basic idea here is that if we somehow rid our minds of all that is even slightly uncertain, we will be left only with absolute knowledge, if anything at all remains. If this seems hard to understand, it helps to realize that Descartes thought of truth as a simple and evident property, a property discernible by the "natural light" of reason, just as a color is discernible by ordinary light. The importance of this visual metaphor is difficult to overestimate, because for Descartes recognition or realization was a form of perception conceived in terms of the model of sight. (Note that while I have spoken and will continue to speak of 'awareness' in general, here, and elsewhere in what follows, 'perception' is used to designate more specific forms of awareness, such as sight.) Supposedly, once we recognize a single undoubtable truth as truth, we have a paradigm, a standard by which to judge all other apparent or possible truths. We can then test potential truths by comparing them with our sample. The parallel here is to comparing colored objects, such as fabric swatches, to a preferred sample. The similarity or lack of similarity between two swatches compared is obvious to us on looking at them, at least in unproblematic cases. Descartes thought that having a single indubitable truth is having a wholly unproblematic sample of truth to which we can then compare other beliefs, just as we compare fabric swatches to test similarity of color. He thought there would be an obvious similarity between two true beliefs, a similarity actually more obvious to reason than the color similarity is to visual perception. A corresponding lack of similarity between a true and a false belief would be equally obvious. As long as we discern just one unquestionably true proposition, then, we can always compare any other belief or claim to it and so judge that claim or belief to be true or false. More specifically, we will know it to be true if it has the same degree of "clarity and distinctness" as the known truth. We will know it to be false, or at least questionable, if it falls short of that standard to any degree.

As a brief sample of the sort of thing one should be very much aware of in reading philosophy, note that the foregoing immediately raises some questions. For instance, the analogy between comparing true beliefs and similarly colored fabric swatches reminds us that often, if the colors are very close, we cannot really tell if two swatches are of the same color or only very similar in color. In such cases we usually have to make a decision, perhaps after some discussion with others. Descartes does not allow for that sort of inconclusive comparison because he characterizes comparisons of the "clarity and distinctness" of ideas made by the "natural light of reason" as always decisive. This should immediately suggest that Descartes is stipulating or assuming rather a lot about intellectual comparisons of beliefs. Additionally, if true beliefs are similar in virtue of recognizable clarity and distinctness shared with obvious truth, what about false beliefs? Are they simply different from true beliefs, but diversely so? Or are false beliefs characterized by a similarity either not mentioned or not thought of by Descartes?

The key part of the Cartesian process of discerning and elaborating knowledge—for Descartes the doing of all moral and physical science—is application of the method of analysis. This is the process of breaking down complex notions into their simple components and testing the truth of each of those components. If each of the various components of a complex notion passes the test for truth, if each component matches the standard of truth in clarity and distinctness, then the truth of the complex notion itself is established. This is the essence of the Cartesian method: to analyze the complex into its simple components, and to test those components by comparing them to an indubitable sample of truth. Only when the various components have been found to be individually true can the aggregate, the original complex notion, be accepted as true. And what is gained thereby is not just the establishment of a single complex notion as true. Once established as true, that complex notion then itself serves as a known, reliable component of even more complex ideas or theories or descriptions. In this way Descartes thought we would eventually build up knowledge as a complete intellectual or ideational mirror-image of reality. Of course human knowledge will always be restricted by the limited nature of our intellects, but Descartes thought that God gave us the ability to know everything that can be of importance to us. Some metaphysical truths, such as the exact nature of God, for instance, must always elude us, but they are not necessary for us to know.

Descartes had a number of secondary objectives. Uppermost among these was to understand the nature of what he called our "ideas," as well as the origins of those ideas. By an "idea" Descartes meant anything present to the mind, anything that is an object of awareness. Thought or thinking just is having ideas: "*Thought* . . . covers . . . everything that exists in us in such a way that we are immediately conscious of it. Thus all operations of the will, intellect, imagination, and of the sense are thoughts. [And] *Idea* is a word by which I understand the form of any thought." (Descartes, *Arguments*, Haldane and Ross, 1969:II:52.) Aside from his egocentric skepticism and analytic method, this was Descartes's most momentous contribution to philosophy. As Richard Rorty (1931–) puts it, "the modern use of the word *idea* derives . . . from Descartes. The novelty was the notion of a single inner space in which bodily and perceptual sensations, mathematical truths, moral rules, the idea of God, moods of depression, and all the rest . . . were objects of quasi-observation." (Rorty, 1979:48–50)

Descartes is quite adamant about what some call the "transparency" of the mind and about the nature of its contents. Descartes explicitly disallows that there might be something in the mind, which can only be an idea in his broad sense, of which we might not be conscious: "nothing can exist in the mind . . . of which [the mind] is not conscious." (Descartes, *Reply to Objections IV*, Haldane and Ross, 1969:II:115) Also, in a 1641 letter to the Reverend Mersenne, Descartes says: "by the term 'idea' I mean in general everything which is in our mind when we conceive of something, no matter how we conceive it." (Kenny, 1970:105) For something to be in the mind, for something to be thought, again in the broadest sense, just is for it to be an idea present to us.

Ideas, then, are the very stuff of awareness, and like everything else, with the sole exception of God, they must arise from something. The point of discovering the origins of what presents itself to the mind is to distinguish between ideas that represent real things and those that do not. For Descartes all ideas are equally potential representations of real things when considered in themselves. And we may entertain any idea, except that of God, while reserving judgment about whether or not it does represent a real thing. Thinking of all the contents of awareness as initially "neutral" ideas, entertained in the intellect but not assented to, enabled Descartes to raise the question about the possible causes of ideas without having to impugn the ideas themselves or to distinguish among them as we tend to do. For example, we are more dubious about something seen dimly through a fog than about the feel of something rough and heavy in our hand. But for Descartes, since ideas are in themselves only the contents of the mind, they cannot, again in themselves, be more or less than what they are as "presentations." The sole exception, as will become evident, is the idea of God. And to have an idea itself seems to have been more or less what we now think of as having a mental image. Descartes's idea of an idea seems to have been closest to what we would describe as imagining something, or more specifically imaging something.

This view of awareness as so many distinct instances of imagining or imaging, then, was a conception of awareness as essentially the having of so many potential representations. To be aware at all was to have something present to the mind on the model of seeing something. It was a further question whether an idea, a presentation, did or did not represent something other than itself: i.e., a possible external cause. Even awareness of one's own body must always be secondary and indirect in the sense of being first direct perception of an idea about the body, and only secondly acceptance of it, or "assent" to it, as a pain or as hunger or as feeling cold. At first Descartes's conception of awareness may seem plausible, for we understand how awareness even of goings-on in our own bodies is a complicated neurophysiological process culminating in parts of the brain. But Descartes's view is very different from this scientific one. For him, even the events in the higher parts of the brain, which we conceive as actually the instantiation of awareness, were only further causes of ideas occurring in a still different realm: the autonomous, nonmaterial, conscious mind.

The assimilation of all cases of awareness to the having of ideas is crucial to Descartes's project, then, because it enables his holistic skepticism by letting him question the veracity of all perceptions without regard to their degree of immediacy or anything else. By locating only ideas, as purely mental occurrences, directly in the mind, Descartes effectively detaches those which are perceptions, even internal bodily perceptions, from their causes. This means that on his scheme no one idea is any different in epistemic status from any other. That is, no one sort of awareness has greater or lesser immediate veracity in the order of knowledge regardless of how it is experienced—again with the exception of the idea of God. All ideas are, in themselves, neutral presentations. Whether some are veridical representations of something other than themselves is a further question. Our tendency, mentioned above, to trust touch more than sight is pointless on Descartes's scheme, wherein touch and sight both initially present equally neutral ideas to the mind. That is, until judged to relate to something real, the ideas are simply the constituents of a thinking mind. This initial neutrality of ideas is also crucial to Descartes's attempt to account for error, as we will see in considering the fourth meditation.

The assimilation of all the contents of awareness to ideas is perhaps one of the most difficult notions to grasp in understanding Descartes. What it implies is that for Descartes, to be a conscious entity is first and foremost to be a pure consciousness entertaining ideas. It must be appreciated fully that the awareness of one's own body, as in the case of having a headache or just flexing one's fingers, was for Descartes just as problematic an idea or set of ideas as the thought that there is a world or that God exists. In other words, all of these ideas stood in need of being grounded or proven to be true. All needed to be shown to be worthy of our belief. That is the point of Descartes's novel egocentric skepticism. The *Meditations*, then, is basically an exercise in showing why we should believe what we already do believe.

If the heart of Cartesian epistemology is egocentric skepticism and ideational representation, the most important metaphysical implication of Descartes's conception of mind and awareness is that we are, each of us, essentially nonspatial singular awarenesses: pure consciousnesses without dimensions, though we have spatial dimensions if we are in fact embodied. As minds, we are not spatial; consciousness is not the sort of thing that takes up room. Other people's bodies, material objects, and even our own bodies are initially ideas we entertain and which must be shown to truly represent realities before they can be taken as actual perceptions. Before we can accept that we do have a body, that there are material objects, and that other people exist, the Cartesian epistemological project must succeed. Otherwise all of alleged human knowledge remains so much unsubstantiated conjecture. The epistemological project, then, is the most pressing issue for intellectual inquiry.

One more point must be made before we turn to the *Meditations*. When you read each of the six meditations, or even excerpts from them, you must read as if you are the author, as if you are Descartes. Every time you read the word "I" it must refer to you, not to Descartes. Otherwise not only does the argument not work, but you will not really understand what Descartes was doing. His project was not only to articulate his arguments for himself, nor to lay them out for others in a purely abstract way. He was in effect writing a guide that everyone could follow to establish basic truths for themselves. It is *you* that may be dreaming, *you* that may be fooled by the evil spirit, and *you* who understands that in the very act of doubting you are asserting your existence. If you read the *Meditations* in the third person, you will only appreciate them as an exercise, as Descartes's contribution to philosophy, and you will never feel their philosophical power or really understand what Descartes thought his meditations achieved or how they supposedly grounded our ordinary beliefs about ourselves and the world. In the following discussions of the various meditations I am careful to speak always in the present tense about Descartes, as I already have to an extent, in order to give the material a more immediate tone. In like manner, do not read what follows as about what was thought more than three hundred years ago; try to read about Descartes as if he were a contemporary with whom you might discuss philosophy.

METHODOLOGICAL DOUBT

W E CAN now proceed with an outline of the structure of the first meditation's argument. After some preliminaries are done, Descartes sets out to doubt the evidence of his senses: "Everything which I have thus far accepted as entirely true . . . has been acquired from the senses or by means of the senses. But I have learned by experience that these senses sometimes mislead me, and it is prudent never to trust wholly those things which have once deceived us." (Descartes, 1:18 [I:145]) Having sometimes failed him, Descartes's senses are now wholly suspect because error shows that there is nothing about individual instances of sense-experience that is self-verifying, hence there can be no certainty gained from sense-experience. Sense-experience has not yet been reduced to so many ideas and their hypothetical causes, but Descartes here makes a move dating back to the skepticism of philosophers such as Pyrrho (360–270 B.C.) and Sextus Empiricus (c. A.D. 200). The move is to dredge up cases in which he has misperceived something and to then generalize on that basis that the senses are not to be trusted. This is to sacrifice the huge bulk of reliable perception because of the tiny possibility of error; but, more significantly, it is to follow in Plato's footsteps and require that knowledge be certain and perfect.

Descartes proceeds by supposing that perhaps he is dreaming and that everything that he seems to see and hear and feel and taste and smell actually is nonexistent and appears to him only in a dream. The point here is to shake his own faith in the reality of sense-experience in a holistic and systematic way, to fully realize that however real things may feel or look, there is always a slight but nonetheless real possibility that they are illusory. Most of us have had the experience of waking from a vivid dream and being surprised by the sudden dissolution of one range of experience and the continuation of another, so Descartes's proposal is not as bizarre as it might otherwise be thought. In any case, his crucial point seems fair enough: it is not so much that we might in fact be dreaming, but that we cannot tell at any given moment whether we are or not. Descartes's claim is that "there are no conclusive indications by which waking life can be distinguished from sleep. . . ." (Descartes, 1:19 [I:146]) The sheer possibility that we may be deceived, that we are actually dreaming while apparently awake, is supposedly enough to impugn all that we seem to be aware of through our senses. There is, however, a more subtle—and competing—reading of the dream argument, which merits mention here not only because it may well be what Descartes actually intended, but also because it illustrates the complexity of philosophical interpretation. It has been argued that rather than challenging our ability to distinguish dreaming and waking states, Descartes is maintaining that we have no reason to believe that effects resemble their causes in the waking state, since they clearly do not in the dreaming state. (Wilson, 1978) We are no better off even when awake, then, with respect to trusting our sense-experience. Therefore, we must suspend judgment even though we might know we are awake. This makes better sense of Descartes's later retraction, in the sixth meditation, in which he says that temporal coherence does enable us to tell the waking from the dreaming state. This second reading is also consistent with the above-quoted passage, because its point then would be that there is nothing about the *waking* state that guarantees the veracity of sense-experience.

Outside of an epistemological context, we find it hard to really understand, while fully awake, what it is to think that we might nonetheless be dreaming, or that what we experience may be as unreliable as what we dream. But we do seem forced to admit the logical possibility that we could "awaken" in the next moment. What this means is only that it is not self-contradictory to say: "Even though I have no reason to think so, I could at this moment actually be dreaming." We can imagine substituting some other condition for the dreaming one, such as being drugged or under the influence of the proverbial mad scientist. The point is just this: we must allow that at any moment our ongoing experience might change so radically that what preceded the change is judged illusory. And this is perhaps enough to support Descartes's point that past error suffices to undermine any certainty we may feel that things are as they appear to be at any given moment.

Assuming acceptance of Descartes's dream hypothesis, it may seem that he has all he needs to clear his mind of everything which can be doubted and so is prepared to discern whatever may be indubitable and therefore undeniably true. That is, whatever remains as an undoubted and undoubtable object of thought must be true. But the dream hypothesis is not really enough to generate the thoroughgoing philosophical doubt Descartes needs, because even if we do come to doubt our senses because of it, we need not doubt our reason. That is, we may think that even if we are fooled by our senses into thinking that there is a certain object before us when there is something else or nothing at all there, we may still feel quite certain about a number of things, such as that five plus five equals ten or that a triangle must have internal angles equaling 180 degrees or that however mistaken we may be about the one pink elephant we seem to see, we still seem to see one and not two or more. The worry is that there are some apparent truths which are not affected by being possibly only dreamt as opposed to grasped in waking life. In the case of five plus five equaling ten, for instance, whether I really add five and five, hallucinate the addition while awake, or only dream the addition, it remains true that five plus five equals ten. Descartes needs to impugn even these truths which seem to be evidently true even in a dream context, that is, which do not seem to be undermined by the context in which they occur.

What Descartes does to carry through his methodological doubt is to imagine that not only do his senses deceive him, but that a very powerful and evil entity, the "evil spirit" or malevolent demon, also deceives his reason. "I will therefore suppose that . . . a certain evil spirit, not less clever and deceitful than powerful, has bent all his efforts to deceiving me." (Descartes, 1:22 [I:148]) Descartes may not understand what it would be for five plus five not to equal ten, but he determines to think that maybe the certainty that it does, as well as his inability to imagine an alternative, are not indications of the truth of the equation but rather are due to the deceptive work of the evil spirit. The point may be clear, but it requires a little expansion to avoid a common misreading. Many take it that Descartes's evil spirit impugns reason in the sense of the process of reasoning. But this is not actually so. If this were the case, it is not clear that Descartes could proceed, for he would face the awesome concern that his actual thinking about his own existence and about the evil spirit and its activities is distorted by the spirit. However, Descartes never quite focuses on reasoning, at least not as we would. This is partly due to his conception of thought not being as active a one as ours is. Remember that Descartes thinks of thinking as the entertaining of ideas, and as becomes evident in the work of the empiricists who followed (Locke, Berkeley and Hume), this is an inherently passive conception of thought. In any case, what the evil spirit impugns is less reasoning than specific ideas such as that the sum of five and five is ten. What Descartes really succeeds in doing, then, is to make problematic a host of ideas he entertains as products of reason, as opposed to products of the senses, which the dream hypothesis takes care of. In a crucial way, Descartes never subjects his ability to reason—that is, to think discursively—to the deceptive influence of the evil spirit. To us, the distinction between reasoning and the products of reason conceived of as so many ideas seems very dubious, but the latter is what the evil spirit makes doubtful. As noted, it is likely that if Descartes thought that the evil spirit impugns the activity of reasoning, he simply could not go further than the first meditation, because the postulation of the evil spirit would preclude that any of the reasoning which follows could yield reliable conclusions. The evil spirit, therefore, is tacitly limited to impugning only those ideas, those products of reason, which Descartes has already found among the objects of his belief.

As noted, what Descartes is doing is trying to doubt everything in order to clear away every belief possible. He thinks that if he succeeds in his methodological doubt, then anything that still remains an object of thought and which he cannot doubt must be true. And once he finds even one such truth, supposedly he will know what truth is like and be able to use that discovered instance of truth as a sample for testing other beliefs. Descartes's thinking here is, at base, surprisingly naive. As noted in a previous section, he assumes that recognizing one case of truth is like seeing something which he will always be able to identify when he sees it again, just on the basis of that first experience. What enables him to think in this way, to feel sure of his ability to recognize truth, is that he not only thinks of truth as a property, but as one which overwhelms us, which imposes itself on us, so that the comparison is to seeing something unique and literally unforgettable. Recall again the im-

portance of visual metaphors in Descartes's thinking to better appreciate how he models recognition of truth on visually recognizing
something (or someone) well known. Descartes never wonders
whether changing circumstances might make a difference to the
identification of truth, because he thinks there are no circumstantial
changes that can affect truth, since truth is and must be objective
and eternal.

In fairness to Descartes, his reliance on visual metaphor in the
conception of thought is not a simplistic one. Many who stress
Descartes's reliance on the visual cast his conception of thought in
rather crude terms because their intent is to stress a juxtaposition
of subject and object. This is in part so they can criticize Descartes
for a naive and problem-generating conception of awareness as
consciousness of so many images—and admittedly Descartes does
say things that support this move: "my thoughts . . . are like images
of objects, and it is to these alone that the name of 'idea' properly
applies." (Descartes, 3:35–36 [I:159]) These critics go on to criticize
that conception for reifying the objects of awareness into so many
image-like ideas. But while there is a great deal of truth to this
criticism, the conception is more imposed than found. Descartes's
major purpose in characterizing the objects of awareness as images
is to assimilate perception to thought, and the real significance of
Descartes's reliance on the visual is not an overemphasis of the
subject-object or percipient-perceived juxtaposition, but rather
that, aside from such phenomena as great pain, in vision we have
a striking sort of experience which fills our awareness. Descartes's
notion was not so much that in thought, as in vision, objects, or
truth, present themselves as a given in juxtaposition to our subjectivity. Rather the notion was that in thought, as in vision, what
we are aware of is wholly immediate and totally commanding of
our attention or consciousness. The real problem is not a simple
equation of objects of awareness with images, but what was noted
earlier, namely, that the images then become *representations* of their
causes and so themselves the proper objects of awareness in whatever mode. This makes the world disappear into a purely inferential
realm.

It is important to understand the lengths to which Descartes
goes in rendering his ordinary beliefs problematic, and why he
feels he can go to those lengths. The central thought underlying
his methodological doubt is that everything that exists or is the case
is the consequence of divine will, as is everything that can be con-

ceived, such as five plus five equaling ten. So five plus five, it turns out, equals ten not because of something inherent in numbers themselves, or in arithmetic as an autonomous phenomenon or as a defined closed system, but because God wills it. Things are as they are, for Descartes, because God wills them to be so. And not only did God create the world as it is by an act of will, he maintains it in existence by an act of continuous creation or continuously willing that the world go on existing. God's responsibility for things being as they are is total. The evil spirit, who really is—for the moment—an otherwise unthinkable malevolent God, can make even the most apparently obvious belief be deceptive, because there is no necessity outside of what God wills to be so. We may not understand how five plus five might equal something other than ten, but because God could have made it so, the evil spirit is capable of deceiving us. When Descartes speaks of the "evil spirit" he is in fact entertaining the theologically risky idea that God might be a deceiver, for the real force of the evil spirit hypothesis is that the demon is able to do anything to deceive Descartes. Otherwise the evil spirit's sole inability, which emerges in the second meditation, would not be so decisive.

Descartes, then, sets out to clear his mind of everything that can possibly be doubted. His hope and conviction are that he will be left with at least a single instance of truth which will stand out in isolation and provide him with a criterion for judging every other belief. And if he succeeds, not only will he have a sample of truth, but, because that sample is the first and most obvious truth he encounters, he will have found the bedrock on which he can ground whatever other knowledge he may have or acquire.

Descartes talks easily about methodological doubt, about systematically taking up a doubtful attitude toward various things he has believed unquestioningly all his life. It is an appropriate and serious question just how realistic it is to try to doubt what one has no reason to doubt, especially the existence of one's own body. Even Descartes realized the implausibility of what he was suggesting, acknowledging the strength of our inclination to believe what seems evident to us. But instead of making things better, he made them worse by saying that to counter that inclination he would think everything he believed to be true to actually be false. This cannot be of any help, since it is harder to think that what one believes is actually false than merely to entertain the abstract possibility that it might be false. Descartes simply does not really address the question of whether we can doubt what we have no real reason to doubt, and so does not legitimate his methodological doubt. Yet it is absolutely crucial to his enterprise that we be able to doubt what we most firmly believe, since without that ability we appear to be psychologically determined to believe what seems evident, and so are unable to do Descartes's sort of philosophy at all. If we are unable to systematically question *all* our beliefs, we cannot discover what Descartes imagines are the grounds of true beliefs, and so cannot determine which constitute absolutely certain knowledge.

So far we have Descartes introducing his methodological doubt and cheating a bit—though certainly not deliberately—by not seriously considering the credibility of doubting the obvious. The goal is to discover one or more basic truths, truths wholly impervious to doubt. But now we have to distance ourselves a little from the introduction of methodological doubt and have a look at what underlies it, and that is the notion of the need for, and possibility of, grounding knowledge on self-evident basic truths. This defining characteristic of Cartesian thought, so-called "foundationalism," is the notion that knowledge is hierarchical, that complex truths are based on and composed of simpler truths, and that those simpler truths are based on and composed of still simpler truths. It is precisely Cartesian foundationalism which underlies Descartes's innovative view that analytic method can yield certain knowledge. Moreover, foundationalism entails not only that knowledge is hierarchical in this simple-to-complex fashion, but that nothing can be accepted as knowledge until we have shown on what it is based, until we have traced its antecedents and established its grounds by unearthing its components and testing each of them for truth or falsity. But foundationalism is not just about degrees of relative fundamentality and simplicity of basic truths. The real point of foundationalism is that when we get to bedrock, when we reach the simplest and most fundamental truths, and so have justified our knowledge claims by showing their grounding, we finally reach truths which are and can only be their *own* justification. These are truths that are not themselves capable of being justified because they are ultimate and self-verifying and serve as their own evidence or authority. However, there is now a complication, because for some foundationalists these most basic truths are propositional; that is, they are articulations, no matter how simple, of elemental facts or states of affairs. But for other foundationalists, particularly Descartes, we do not really reach the end of justification, of grounding, until we get past all articulations to an "intuition," a direct awareness of a simple self-verifying actuality such as the law of noncontradiction. (The law of noncontradiction bars assertion of both P and not-P, where 'P' is any proposition capable of being true or false, on pain of incoherence.)

Foundationalism, or this view that knowledge is an inverted pyramid resting on fundamental truths and principles, is very much at odds with the contemporary view that there are various different sorts of knowledge, that not everything can be demonstrated to be based on something else, and that we do not understand what it is for something to be self-evident or self-justifying. It is especially at odds with the contemporary view that only other propositions justify propositions. This point is difficult to make in the context of an introductory work, but it has a certain intuitive clarity, and is that the relationship existing between X and Y, where X is said to justify Y, is one that can only hold between like things, which is to say it can only hold between linguistic items: in particular, between sentences. Descartes thought that there could be a relation of justification between an actuality, for instance an existent God, and an idea, and that the disparity in nature or kind did not weaken or preclude the justificatory relationship. It is fundamental for Descartes that knowledge must be grounded on the simplest, most certain truths or evidence. And the linguistic appears to be once removed from the real, so the notion is that the most basic truths are not true sentences or propositions but actualities properly and directly represented or "given" in true ideas. Later the empiricists were to hold that these given actualities were sensory data, but whether for Descartes or Locke, the notion is that what grounds or justifies belief, and so makes it knowledge, is something nonlinguistic, an actuality immediately present to the mind. This notion is now almost universally rejected. Donald Davidson, one of the most important philosophers of our time, maintains that "nothing can count as a reason for holding a belief except another belief." (Davidson, 1986:310) Davidson expands this by saying that "knowledge depend[s] on experience, and experience ultimately on sensation. But this is the 'depend[s]' of causality, not of evidence or justification." (Davidson, 1986:313–14) And in addition to argued rejections of Descartes's notion, it is not very clear just what a basic, self-evident, nonlinguistic or nonpropositional truth *is*. As we proceed through the *Meditations* it will become clear that this lack of clarity about a central notion in the argument is important. What will begin to emerge is that what is most notably missing is any notion of the role of *conceptualization*, something that would not really enter the picture until Kant. That is, what is missing is the understanding that something "given" to consciousness is not *as such* an object of cognition or reflective awareness, that what is given to consciousness must first be interpreted as a this or a that—i.e., brought under some concept. Descartes proceeds as if mere givenness suffices. In any case, in Cartesian foundationalism so long as each elemental component of each complex truth is itself a grounded or justified truth, and known to be such, or is directly traced to such truth, then even the most complex proposition, such as a highly complicated description of an elaborate natural process, would itself be certain and, more importantly, would be known to be true. It would seem that some of the foundational truths must be propositional, but each would be the barest articulation of an evident actuality faithfully represented. It is almost as if the barest articulations of truly represented actualities are not descriptions at all but more like acknowledgements, as a nod is significant though not verbal. This is how the ambiguity between the factual and the propositional seems to be glossed, namely, by thinking of some uses of language as somehow too basic to be problematic. But more likely what is happening is that given Descartes's assimilation of thought to the having of image-like ideas, at this basic level language, especially descriptive language, simply drops out and apprehension of the simplest self-verifying truths *just is* having a specific, minimal idea. This consideration of foundationalism and of the rather mysterious nature of Cartesian foundations should alert one to how we run into trouble even in the very first meditation, and how what Descartes sets out to establish in the *Meditations* is itself problematic, whatever we may decide about how he tries to establish it.

We can sum things up as follows: in the first meditation Descartes supposedly clears the way for perception of self-evident truth by doubting everything he can doubt, using the dream and evil spirit devices to cast doubt on the evidence of his senses and on any beliefs that seem to be truths of reason. Implicit in all this is the foundationalist idea that we must trace everything we believe to its most basic roots, and that those roots must be further analyzed into their basic components and each resulting component individually tested for truth. Only then can we accept a belief as a case of knowledge, and only then can we proceed to consider and acquire more complex beliefs.

In considering the first meditation, I have focused on the most epistemologically important points. It is necessary to see that Descartes's doubt initially encompasses everything, including his very existence. Once that is appreciated, it is easier to understand just how fundamental Cartesian doubt must be, and it is also easier to begin to understand the thoroughgoing nature of epistemological considerations. Doubt is not epistemological unless it is radical, unless it goes to the very core of its object. When Descartes begins to doubt in an epistemological mode, he cannot stop short of doubting whether he himself exists as a doubter.

Supposedly the desired consequence of the radical epistemological doubt of the first mediation is that it will sweep away everything except what is totally invulnerable to doubt in virtue of its self-evident and inviolable truth. At the end of the first meditation, then, we are poised to discover any surviving belief or proposition which, by virtue of having survived, will prove immune to doubt and thus serve as the keystone of epistemology.

THE *COGITO*

The structure of the second meditation is somewhat more complex than that of the first, largely because what it contains, in spite of being less radical than the notion of doubting everything, is considerably more complex in conception. Basically, in the second meditation Descartes derives the idea of an existent, autonomous mind from his undeniable experience of thinking and doubting. In other words, the very doubting that is initiated in the first meditation is used in the second to manifest not only the obvious existence of the thinking and doubting, but also the existence of a thinker and doubter. The thinking which manifests this existence is construed as a defining property of what exists, and so as presumably manifesting the existence of a mind to which the property of thought belongs and which that property therefore defines.

Somewhat differently put, Descartes maintains that thinking cannot exist just as free-floating thought, that it is a property of something, that it is generated by something, and that that something is a mind. In the very act of doubting or thinking is the realization that doubting or thinking entails existence. But for Descartes realization of that existence is not just reflexive awareness of the existence of the doubting and thinking. Descartes immediately moves to the idea that the doubting or thinking, since they supposedly cannot exist in themselves, must be the doubting and thinking of a substantive mind. That is, they must be repeatedly occurring but individually transient properties of a mind that persists and is independent of any particular act of doubting or think-ing. But as will be stressed below, this substantial mind is not identical with an embodied person. It is a "pure" mind. What makes it substantial is that it is not merely identical with any given thought or set of thoughts but is something which *has* thoughts. In other words, a mind is not a property of anything; it is a substance capable of itself having properties, and the defining property it has is thought.

In the second meditation Descartes also claims to derive the idea of matter or what he calls "extension," thus establishing that aside from mental substance, the existence of which is evident in his own thought, a second substance, matter, is possible. It is ex-tension or matter that the intellect grasps or understands as the common element in ideas of varied objects, and that, as the common element, may be actually real and so be the cause of some ideas. But it is only the concept of extension which Descartes derives; the actual existence of extended matter is still to be proven. It emerges, then, that there is more going on than Descartes reassuring himself that he does in fact exist. Aside from doing epistemology, Descartes is also doing metaphysics, because he draws conclusions about the nature of what his methodological doubt establishes. That is, not only does he note that methodological doubt establishes the basic truth that he exists when he doubts or thinks, he also draws con-clusions about the nature of that which thinks and about the nature of that which does not think but nonetheless may exist. What thinks is *mind*, a special "stuff" that has the one defining property which he experiences directly, namely, thought. What does not think, and may exist, and is defined by the property of being extended, is matter.

As suggested, care must be taken not to confuse the establish-ment of the existence of mind and the derivation of the concept of matter with demonstration of the existence of Descartes as an entity which both thinks and is embodied. What is proven to exist in the act of reflective thinking or doubting is a thinking mind, not Descartes as an embodied entity. The point is that thinking suffices to establish the actual existence of mind, because thought is the defining property of mind, and since thought is plainly taking place as Descartes thinks and doubts, his mind must exist. But with matter things are rather different. As emerges in the case of the wax experiment, being extended is the defining property of matter or extension, but that defining property is not directly evident to Descartes as is his own thought. It is perfectly possible that when he considers the property of being extended he is either dreaming or being fooled by the evil spirit. Matter is not proven to exist in the second meditation; it is only the concept of matter, the idea of matter, that is established.

If this last point is unclear, think of the following example: you may return home and conclude that someone broke in while you were away because you do not remember leaving things as you find them. You reason as follows: if you did not in fact leave things as you found them, then someone entered your home. If someone did break in, that would explain why things are as they are. You have the idea of a possible intruder, and it is an idea that does a certain amount of explanatory work: it would explain why things are as they are. However, it is possible, though perhaps unlikely, that you yourself moved things around and then forgot having done so. If you forgot how you left things, that would also explain why things are as you found them. All you have, then, is the possibility, even the likelihood, that how you found things means that an intruder was there. But you have no conclusive proof that anyone else actually was in your home so long as it is possible that you yourself are responsible for how you found things. In like manner, at the end of the second meditation, Descartes will have enough reason to think that the behavior of a piece of wax with which he experiments is explicable if matter really does exist and continues to be extended even though its form changes. But that behavior is also explicable if the series of ideas he has about the wax are only a consistent sequence in a dream or the equally consistent but deceptive products of the evil spirit. Nonetheless, just as you have the thought of a possible intruder, as one adequate explanation of how you found things, after the second meditation Descartes has the thought of matter as an adequate explanation of why he has just the series of ideas he has when he manipulates the wax as he does.

We have, then, two major points made in the second meditation: the direct experience of thinking provides the idea of a defining property which supposedly establishes that mind exists, and manipulation of a common object establishes that no matter how it may change, matter continues to be extended. This latter constitutes the derivation of the concept of matter from a series of experiences, and that suffices to establish that there may really be something that does in fact continue to be extended even through radical transformation: in short, matter may exist.

Let us now look a little more closely at these two most central points. With respect to his own existence, essentially what Descartes does is offer a reconstruction of the obvious. That is, he does no more than point out that so long as one is thinking, one exists. And reflection on this point, recognition of how one must exist to think, provides him with an incontrovertible truth: "*I am, I exist*, is necessarily true every time that I pronounce it or conceive it in my mind." (Descartes, 2:24 [I:150]) The force behind this intuition is that it is undoubtable. Descartes speaks of the necessary truth of his intuition because in the very act of thinking or doubting his existence he demonstrates that existence. Not even God, temporarily disguised as the evil spirit, can make it so that Descartes is deceived that he exists while he does not exist.

And do not confuse this constraint on God or the evil spirit with a limitation of our finite imagination, and so as something that still allows a margin for error or deception. That is, do not think that it is just a matter of our being unable to imagine how it might be done and that God or the evil spirit might indeed be able to make Descartes not exist while he doubts his own existence. The point is that for Descartes to not exist while thinking or deceived about his existence would be for Descartes to both exist and not exist at the same time, and that is a logical contradiction, not merely a very difficult possibility falling outside our imaginative limits. There is simply nothing that could count as both existing—in order to think—and not existing at the same time. But there are real questions raised by Descartes's claim. For instance, something Descartes never considers is whether he continues to be the numerically identical being while sporadically or intermittently thinking or doubting over even a very short period of time. If God were to annihilate and recreate Descartes moment after moment, but with all the memories of his previous instantiation, there would be a sense in which, though existent in each instant of thinking or doubting, Descartes's apparently continuous existence would be a sham because it would not be the actual continuous existence of the numerically same mind. And this is only a possibility which occurs to our finite minds. An omnipotent God would have many other ways of achieving the same end without attempting to violate the logical impossibility of making Descartes exist and not exist at the same time.

Descartes manages to complicate things in several ways, but the first thing to understand is that he thinks he has found his absolute starting point. The most basic truth available to him is his own existence while thinking. Assertion of his own existence while he is thinking is absolutely incorrigible: he cannot be wrong because to think is to exist: "I am, I exist . . . I am now admitting nothing except what is necessarily true." (Descartes, 2:26 [I:152]) But while it is true enough that Descartes must exist to think or doubt, re-member that existence here does not apply to Descartes as an em-bodied person, which brings us to an important difficulty alluded to in earlier remarks about how Descartes conceives of thought as the defining property of substantive mind. The fact is that all is not as smooth as Descartes would have it. He makes a quite ille-gitimate move when he goes from the admittedly certain fact that while he thinks he exists—at least as the ongoing thinking—to his further claim that he is a *thing* that thinks, that he exists as a thinking thing. No argument is offered here, only a gloss: "I am something real and really existing, but what thing am I? [A] thing which thinks." (Descartes, 2:26 [I:152]) But while there is a problem here, it bears repetition that a very common mistake is to read this con-clusion as Descartes meaning 'thing' to refer to himself as embod-ied. 'Thing' does *not* here mean a material thing. What Descartes is concluding is that he is a *mental* thing that thinks, a substantive mind. (If it helps, think of the Cartesian mind as a soul, which, for him, it in fact is.) The existence of matter is still problematic. Too many readers of the second meditation initially read 'thing' as 'ma-terial thing', and in spite of repeated warnings and clarifications, many will find the idea of a mental substance too strange and be inclined to believe that Descartes must be attributing his thinking to a person as a material thing.

Once we are clear on the possible misconstrual of "thing which thinks," we can proceed to consider more thoroughly that while Descartes has all the warrant he needs to say that thought is taking place, and so that he exists as that thinking, he does not have warrant to say that the thought that is taking place attaches as a property to some (mental) thing that thinks. Put differently, he cannot move from the obvious fact that he is thinking to his claim that he is a thinking thing, for being a thing is not something that is warranted by his realization that thought exists while he thinks or doubts. We may not understand how thought might occur by itself, but that does not matter. Descartes cannot validly conclude that he is a thinking thing from the fact that he is thinking. The trouble is that, as has been stressed, Descartes is assuming that thought is a property, and that as a property thought must attach to something other than itself, just as weight cannot exist by itself but must always be the weight of something. Nor is Descartes's error a silly mistake; it is perfectly natural to construe saying that he exists when he thinks as saying that he exists as a thinking being, something that is distinct from the thinking and which engages in thought. However, this is strictly speaking an illegitimate assumption. Descartes's entire existence could be exhausted by his thinking; his thinking could be the whole of his existence as an autonomous phenomenon not attached to anything else.

But notice that while he makes an unwarranted inference about being a thing which thinks, Descartes does not make the mistake noted above of jumping to the conclusion that in being a thinking thing he is an embodied mind, a physical organism with the ability to think. However, this is actually less because Descartes avoids a mistake than because Descartes actually *begins* with the idea that the thing which thinks is a mental (or spiritual) substance. As such, mind could exist as mental stuff even if no matter at all existed. Descartes never goes beyond saying that the thinking thing is only a mind because it is one of the most basic aims of the second meditation to distinguish mind and body as different substances. Part of the point of establishing the certain existence of mind as manifest in thinking or doubting is to demonstrate that it differs in nature from matter, the existence of which is not proven until the sixth meditation. The existence of Descartes's physical body is just as problematic until the sixth meditation as is the existence of other bodies.

In connection with establishing the existence of mind, Descartes is anxious that one not think the reference to his (to your) existence is a conclusion drawn on evidence, namely, the thinking or doubting. For him, his own existence as a thinking being is not something which he infers on the basis of thought as a premise, and which he then articulates as a conclusion. Rather Descartes directly intuits his existence in the act of thinking or doubting. Here again we encounter the problem of the nature of basic, self-verifying truths. The articulation or "conception" of "I think, I exist" seems to be not a sentence or proposition thought but a simple idea had. Descartes's existence, then, is a fundamental actuality which is not mediated by reasoning or couched in language in being understood: it is somehow directly known. The importance of this is that if assertion of one's own existence were essentially propositional and a conclusion, an inference based on evidence itself distinct from that inference, the assertion could be challenged. Even if it is not immediately clear how we might do it, we might question the validity of the move from realization to description, from even immediate evidence to conclusion, from thought to existence. Instead, then, Descartes insists that "I think, I am" is an intuition. His point is that he does not conclude that he exists from the fact that he is thinking, but rather that as he thinks the thought that he is thinking or doubting, he manifests the actuality of his existence to himself in his act of thinking. The articulation of this, "I think, I exist," seems to be incidental and necessitated only by the fact that he is writing out his meditation.

This intuition, then, is Descartes's first wholly undoubtable truth: the one thing that the dream and evil spirit hypotheses cannot even begin to make questionable. Even dreaming manifests existence in being awareness of a sort, and not even the evil spirit could succeed in deceiving what does not exist. This fundamental intuition is often called the "*cogito*," from the Latin "*cogito, sum*" ("I think, I am") or "*cogito, ergo sum*" ("I think, therefore I am"). Note that the latter formulation, "I think, therefore I am," which is used in the earlier *Discourse on Method*, is argumentative because of the 'therefore.' In the *Meditations* the intuition is articulated simply as "I think, I am" to highlight that "I am" is not a conclusion reached but something realized as immediately evident.

But even if we grant the existence of mind, what of matter? Descartes's argument here is somewhat more subtle, because, as we have seen, what is established about matter at this point is not its existence but the coherency of the concept of matter, hence its possible existence. Descartes proceeds by experimenting with a piece of beeswax, as alluded to above. He looks at the piece of wax, noting its shape; he smells it, noting a faint flowery fragrance; he touches it to his tongue and detects a slight honey flavor; he raps it on the table, noting the dull sound it makes; he feels its texture, noting its irregular and somewhat greasy surface. He then considers carefully how the wax changes utterly when it is heated: it loses its shape, it can no longer be rapped on the table because of its semi-liquid state, its odor changes or is intensified, etc. But Descartes realizes that in whatever state, the wax continues to be extended.

It may seem that what Descartes has done is no more than realize that matter is conserved through change, but this is at least misleading. Our conception of the conservation of matter and energy is that there is no annihilation in transformation. But Descartes is treating the wax as if it consisted of an essence and contingent properties. This is in keeping with the Aristotelian idea that substances must be composed of some essential and some "accidental" features, the former being unchangeable without altering the nature of the thing in question, and the latter being changeable without affecting that nature. For instance, for Aristotle a person is essentially a rational being, and only accidentally five or six feet tall. This easy distinction between essences and accidents is highly problematic. The core of the idea is that there is a difference in kind between essences and accidents, but it is certainly arguable that enough change in something's "accidental" properties amounts to "essential" change. It is also arguable that what counts as an essential property is a function of particular interests. We will not pursue this point, intriguing though it is, but it is important to appreciate that Descartes does not question the essence/accident distinction. He is not using the contemporary notion that matter and energy are conserved in being transformed one into the other; rather he thinks that extension is in itself an essential property. The importance of this has to do with the fact that what he thinks he achieves with the wax example is that after careful analysis of the changes in the wax he has derived the idea that common to all of the wax's accidental forms is the one essential feature of being extended:

> this wax was neither that sweetness of honey, nor that . . . odor of flowers, nor that whiteness, nor that shape, nor that sound, but only a body which a little while ago appeared to my senses under these forms and which now makes itself felt under others. But what is it, to speak precisely, that I imagine . . . in this fashion? Let us consider it attentively and, rejecting everything that does not belong to the wax, see what remains. Certainly nothing is left but something extended. . . . (Descartes, 2:29–30 [I:154])

One important aspect of the wax's extended nature is that its extendedness is something evident only after reflection on the changes the wax may undergo. It is not something that is itself perceivable; extendedness is not itself an object of sense experience. When we see something with width, breadth, and depth, we always see its properties. We do not just see foot-long-ness; we see a yellow ruler the length, breadth, and thickness of which are available to us directly as a colored shape, and only reflectively as extension. But what is most important about all this, at least at the present juncture, is that mind *is* available to us directly as its defining property, namely, our own thought. Therefore, there may be something which is *unlike* mind but is nonetheless real. Descartes is known as a "dualist" because he believed there are two basically different kinds of substances: mind and matter. There is, in effect, a third substance, one that is distinctive because it is self-created, namely, God. However, in the first and second meditations the crucial points are the establishment of the absolutely certain existence of mind as one autonomous substance, and the derivation of the idea of matter or extension as a second possible autonomous substance. But remember that what is demonstrated is the concept of matter, hence its possible existence. It could still be that the reality of matter is only an illusion.

There is need now to touch on a very complex issue that we will not pursue, both because of its difficulty and its marginal relevance to our immediate interests. Notice that above I have been careful to speak of matter as being extended, as Descartes does, and not used the likelier phrase that matter "takes up space." The reason for this is that Descartes has neither a Newtonian concept of absolute space nor an Einsteinian concept of relative space. In fact, he has no concept of space at all. The material universe is a plenum: there is no empty space in it. The reason is that matter, or that which is not mind, is extended; its essence, what makes it a substance, is that it is extended. But it is not extended in space, for to be real something must either be a mind or extension, or, of course, the divine substance of God. Space, as a Newtonian absolute, is not extended in Descartes's sense, so it does not exist. What there is, is either mind or extended matter. Empty space is not a reality, because there could be no empty space except as *another* substance. And regardless of how difficult the idea may seem, Descartes is quite consistent in disallowing the existence of empty space. If matter were in space, space would have to be something distinct from extension, and so exist as a separate substance. What appears to us as space is so many instances of extension. Simple air is material, is extended, and is usually the extension of what appears to us to be empty. (Note that I did not say air fills what appears empty.) Descartes went to some pains to establish that however rarefied stuff might be, as in the case of air or the subtlest gas, it is still material, and as such it is extension in itself, not something else extended in space. (Smith, 1962:65–73)

In this connection, one should not be misled by Descartes's own references to space, as when he speaks of the lines of a geometric figure enclosing a space. In these cases reference is only to what contrasts with determinate objects, such as drawn lines forming a triangle. In any case, as noted, the issue here is a deep metaphysical one, involves notions which are not obviously coherent, and is mentioned only to caution and intrigue the reader. But to this end, to hint further at the deeper complexity of the impossibility of empty space, consider that since a thing may move from point A to point B, but there is no space for it to move in, it seems that motion must *itself* be a separate substance which "combines" with extended objects when they change place. Motion cannot be a property of extended matter, because then nothing could ever be still. But if it is only sometimes "combined" with extended matter, motion must be something in itself. However, tempting though it may be to puzzle over these very arcane aspects of Descartes's thought, our objective here is to understand the basics of the *Meditations*, not to explore metaphysical possibilities. (If these questions do seem intriguing, consult Smith, 1962.)

To sum up, then, the first and second meditations establish, through methodological doubt, that mind exists necessarily when there is thought, and that the ideas we have of material objects, which may or may not exist, enable the derivation of extension as their common essential feature. Mind just is that which thinks; matter just is that which is extended. As noted, a major problem in the first meditation is the credibility of methodological doubt as a possible device; a major problem in the second meditation is that Descartes illegitimately goes from the evident reality of thinking to the assumed reality of something that is doing the thinking: in other words, Descartes assumes that thinking is the property of some substantial mental thing. Many newcomers to philosophy find it very difficult to understand how something could be substantial, a substance, and not be material, since the common use of "substantial" means something like being solid. But all "substantial" and "substance" mean for Descartes is that something is independently existent, that it is not a property of anything else. Aside from owing its existence to God, the mind is a substance in just this sense: it is a primary stuff.

In spite of difficulties, Descartes does seem to have advanced his project. He began by trying to doubt everything, and finds he cannot doubt that while he doubts he exists. Somewhat less convincingly, he derives a common essence of ideas which present themselves to him as material objects: they are extended. He has, then, the needed sample of truth: his "intuition" that while he is thinking he necessarily exists. He has a distinction between mind and matter. And he has the possibility of explaining everything that is present to his mind, his ideas, as effects of material or extended objects. But Descartes's universe at this point is very limited: it contains only his mind (your mind, as you re-enact his meditations) and possibly extended matter. He now must intensify his efforts and consider what else he may come to know with certainty.

THE EXISTENCE OF GOD

DESCARTES begins the third medita-
tion with what amounts to a useful summary of what he thinks he
has achieved in the first two. He does this in order to make clear
the starting point of his reasoning about God, but his remarks are
worth quoting at length because they help us to better understand
a number of things: first, it is made clear what he takes to have
been accomplished by the first two meditations, what he now knows
with certainty; second, we are given a better picture of how he
conceives of consciousness and its contents; third, we appreciate
the tight progressive structure of the *Meditations*.

> Now I shall close my eyes, I shall stop my ears, I shall disregard my
> senses, I shall even efface from my mind all the images of corporeal
> things; or at least, since that can hardly be done, I shall consider them
> vain and false. By thus dealing only with myself and considering what
> is included in me, I shall try to make myself, little by little, better
> known and more familiar to myself. I am a thing which thinks, that
> is to say, which doubts, which affirms, which denies, which knows a
> few things, which is ignorant of many, which wills, which rejects, which
> imagines also, and which senses. For as I have previously remarked,
> although the things which I sense and which I imagine are perhaps
> nothing at all apart from me . . . I am nevertheless sure that those
> modes of thought which I call sensations and imaginations, only just
> as far as they are modes of thought, reside and are found with certainty
> in myself. And in this short statement I think I have reported all that
> I truly know. . . . (Descartes, 3:33 [I:157])

The third meditation tells us a bit more about the nature of mind, but its main job is to establish the existence of God. Recall that in order to get his methodological doubt off the ground Descartes uses two devices: the dream hypothesis to render the products of sense-experience questionable, and the evil spirit hypothesis to render the products of reason questionable. This means that he has established very demanding standards with respect to knowledge claims: anything claimed must be capable of proof that is conclusive in spite of the doubts raised by his two hypotheses. Given that he now wants to prove something positive, in this case the existence of God, Descartes must rebut his skepticism by offering arguments that are conclusive. He must, in short, produce arguments with conclusions as certain as his intuition of his own existence, which serves as the model of truth. In the third meditation he begins by offering a causal argument for the existence of God, an argument which turns on the principle that a cause must be "adequate" to its effect. This principle ultimately derives from the early Greek dictum that nothing can come from nothing—that nothing can come to exist without a cause—and was a notion also central to scholastic thought in the medieval period. Descartes proceeds to use the adequate-cause principle to establish God's existence.

The causal argument is, briefly, that the only possible source of the idea of God is God himself, because no other cause can be adequate to produce the idea of a perfect being. At least this is what Descartes wants us to accept. He begins his argument by reviewing the sorts of ideas he has and their possible sources. It is important to understand how the ideas arise, and Descartes notes that "some seem to be born with me, others . . . to come from without, and the rest to be made . . . by myself." (Descartes, 3:36 [I:160]) Again in a letter to Mersenne, also written in 1641, Descartes draws this three-way distinction somewhat more technically: ideas may be "*adventitious*, such as the idea we . . . have of the sun; *others are constructed or factitious* [like] the idea which the astronomers have of the sun by their reasoning; and *others are innate, such as the idea of God, mind, body, triangle, and . . . those which represent . . . eternal essences*." (Kenny, 1970:104) Chief among the possibilities regarding the origins of ideas is that Descartes is himself the source of some of them, in the sense that he either conjures up an idea, though possibly unknowingly, or puts together a number of ideas to produce a single complex one. For instance, the idea of a unicorn can be understood as a compilation of the distinct ideas of a horse and of a golden horn. But it is crucial to his reflections on ideas and their possible sources that as effects of something, ideas cannot be greater than their causes: "the light of nature makes me clearly recognize that ideas in me are like paintings or pictures, which can, truly, easily fall short of the perfection of the original from which they have been drawn, but which can never contain anything greater or more perfect." (Descartes, 3:40 [I:163])

The central notion here is initially plausible and relates fairly closely to accepted contemporary scientific principles. Basically the notion is that if X produces Y, then Y cannot have more power or content than is found in X. Consider throwing a snowball. The thrown snowball can travel no further than the impetus received allows it to travel, nor can it impact on something with more force than that impetus and its mass jointly produce. Consider now rolling that same snowball down a steep, snowy hillside. By the time the snowball hits the base of the hill, it will have the mass it originally had, plus whatever impetus it gained from gravity and the additional mass of snow picked up in rolling down the hill. When it hits, then, it may well have a great deal more force than it started out with, and the effect it has may be major, such as leveling a cabin. But we would not be tempted to say, except as a joke, that the cabin was leveled by a snowball, because we understand how the cause of the cabin's destruction was a cumulative one and not only the force of the original snowball. The cause of the effect, the destruction of the cabin, must be at least equal to that effect. This is the sort of thinking that Descartes is engaging in when he argues as he does, and we have no trouble understanding it.

However, with respect to God, Descartes is arguing from known effect to inaccessible cause. Basically, it is the lack of alternative adequate sources for the idea of God that supposedly establishes that of necessity the only possible source of the idea is an existent God. And in describing this cause, Descartes provides us with a short list of God's major perfections: "By the word 'God' I mean an infinite substance, independent, omniscient, omnipotent, and that by which I myself and all other existent things . . . have been created and produced." (Descartes, 3:43 [I:165]) However, what is crucial to the argument is that "these attributes are . . . so great and so eminent that the more attentively I consider them, the less I can persuade myself that I could have derived them from my own nature. And consequently we must necessarily conclude . . . that God exists." (Descartes, 3:43 [I:165]) We can clarify the argument by considering what it does *not* claim. To accept Descartes's argument we must accept that we do have the idea of a perfect God. We might be tempted to think, then, that what is required is a perfect idea of God, an idea which discursively and exhaustively captures God's essence, and that it is only as such that the idea of God requires a perfect cause. But this seems not to be the case. Consider a parallel: we have the idea that the series of natural numbers is an infinite series, so we have the idea of an infinite series. That sounds impressive until we realize that what we actually have is the idea that whatever number we count up to, we can always add one or double it or add fifty, and so on. We are in no way tempted to think that somehow there must be something existent which is an infinite series to provide the source of this idea. The point is that the idea of an infinite series is, as we might put it, a functional or performative one: it is an idea of something we can do to any natural number, namely, increase it. We would not be willing to grant Descartes that we have a perfect idea of a perfect being, not if that means that we fully grasp that perfection or that our idea of God is in some sense perfect. In any case, Descartes is well aware of the problem. In a 1642 letter to Regius, Descartes maintained that "the argument is based not on the essence of the idea, by which it is only a mode existing in the human mind and therefore no more perfect than a human being, but on its objective perfection. . . ." (Kenny, 1970:133) All Descartes requires is that we have, for instance, the idea that God is the creator of *all* things. Given the idea that God, as creator of all things, is wholly responsible for the existence of everything and is responsible for maintaining everything in existence, then Descartes would appear to have an idea requiring God as its cause, but not one which is a perfect idea of God.

To recapitulate, any idea we entertain in our minds has a certain reality just insofar as it is an idea and is an object of consciousness. And that in-the-mind reality requires an external cause adequate to its effect. And note that against contemporary usage, Descartes calls this in-the-mind reality, the reality of an idea as an object of thought, the "objective" reality of the idea, where we would speak of its *subjective* reality. When Descartes speaks of subjective reality, he means the reality of the cause of the idea. Consider: "*an idea is the thing thought of itself, in so far as it is objectively in the understanding.*" (Descartes, *Reply to Objections I*, Haldane and Ross, 1969:II:9) The point here is that an idea in the mind is an *object* of thought: it is that on which thought is directed, and as such it has just the reality it has as an ideational object. Since there is, for Descartes, no direct awareness of anything other than ideas, what is outside the mind can only be the *subject* of an idea, in the same sense that a person is the subject of a portrait of that person. But the objective or ideational reality of ideas nonetheless demands adequate causes, so those subjects are the causes of ideas. Of course, with the exception of the idea of God, the mere existence of an idea as an object of thought does not mean that its cause exists as the idea seems to represent it. Recall that when Descartes is moving from the dream hypothesis to the evil spirit hypothesis, he speaks of how ideas of bodies in our dreams are of existents. What he means there is not, as beginning students often think, that what we dream of must be caused by what is real. Descartes cannot mean that because he has not yet established that matter exists. His point is that what we dream cannot be wholly new and must arise from our waking experience. Even what we dream must have a cause, but our waking experience may not be of *real* things; it may be only of so many more ideas, albeit ideas having greater objective reality, i.e., ideas which are more distinct and determinate and so more real as objects of awareness. Nonetheless, these would suffice to cause our dream ideas. In the case of the idea of God, though, its objective reality is supposedly such that its cause *must* be real.

The upshot, then, is that any idea we entertain must have a cause, an origin or source, and supposedly in the case of the idea of God, the nature of the idea is such that only an actual, existent, perfect God could be that source. The way Descartes puts his argument has a measure of effectiveness when we think in terms of the reality an idea has as an object of consciousness, because he is maintaining that whatever degree of objective reality an idea may have must derive from something other than itself, just as everything must not only have a cause but an adequate cause. We tend to collaborate in the argument by thinking of ideas as effects, so it does seem reasonable to maintain further that the idea of a perfect being has to have an adequate cause, and that the only possible adequate cause is the perfect being the idea is an idea of. So the very having of the idea of a perfect being seems to mean that there must be a perfect being to be the cause of the idea. What Descartes wants us to accept is that in having the idea of a perfect being, we have an idea that requires perfection as its cause, but the problem is with accepting that the idea of God is a single effect. That is not something to be accepted too readily.

What is most important about the third meditation is that in offering a causal proof for the existence of God, Descartes reveals a good deal about how he conceives of the contents of the mind. Clearly those contents are taken as individual effects, which must raise questions about the nature of their causes and their relation to their causes. In this regard, the idea of God and its allegedly perfect cause are simply a case in point. What is most significant is that Descartes sets the scene for hundreds of years of epistemology by making it necessary to determine how faithful our internal ideas, as individual, representational effects, are to their external causes. Descartes succeeds in making the assessment of beliefs as cases of knowledge a matter of establishing the representational accuracy of ideas to their causes. Trying to prove the existence of God by appealing to the necessary nature of the cause of the idea of God is only a special case of trying to demonstrate that our ideas are—or at least can be—precise and reliable representations of the world, and that is what Descartes makes the top priority for epistemology in particular and for modern philosophy in general. Our interest in the argument for God's existence given in the third meditation, then, is less in the hoary question of whether there is a God, or even in the precise way Descartes tries to prove there is; our interest is in better understanding how Descartes thought about ideas and their relation to the world.

Discussion of the third meditation would be incomplete without mention of the charge of circularity against Descartes, and it is in this connection that we must consider again the adequate-cause notion. The well-known "circle" charge is that Descartes's causal argument for the existence of God presupposes what is not argumentatively established in the *Meditations*, namely, precisely the adequate-cause principle on which he relies. Something like the premise "causes must be at least as great as their effects" is being assumed, and if the evil spirit might still be deceiving Descartes, then it is just this sort of assumption that should be most problematic. The way to justify such an assumption would be to show that God would not deceive us about anything, and particularly not about notions so fundamental to effective reasoning with respect to the world and God's own reality. But to have that guarantee, Descartes needs to prove the existence of an all-good God. And to prove the existence of an all-good God, at least through the argument offered here, Descartes needs the assumption he is making.

There is some reason to feel, at the end of the third meditation, that the doubts raised in the first meditation have been perhaps too easily resolved. As we shall see when we consider the argument for God's existence offered in the fifth meditation, Descartes does not again offer anything as compelling as the proof of his own existence. If we waive the problems about moving from thinking to being a thinking thing, the intuition of Descartes's own existence stands out as a coercive point, and begins to look less like a sample of self-evident truth than as the sole evident truth Descartes discerns.

ERROR

MEDITATION four is mainly designed to deal with a problem that arises for Descartes from his conception of the contents of the mind as so many ideas, some of which may be representations of an external reality. First, his conception is one that generates a difference between what is in the mind, what is immediately evident to awareness, and an allegedly external world which is somehow rendered inaccessible in any direct way because it is only evidenced or represented in the mind by ideas construed as facsimiles of bits of the world. But, secondly, because most ideas are effects of extended objects, they cannot be precisely like those objects. Here Descartes follows Galileo and precedes Locke in recognizing that the qualities we sense as color, sound, texture (including heat and cold), odor and taste are effects in us of properties of objects quite unlike those effects as they are experienced. Descartes maintains that qualities we experience, such as color or heat, "can be explained without the need to suppose anything in their matter other than . . . motion, size, shape, and arrangement of its parts." (Descartes, *The World*, Cottingham, 1985:89) For example, the searing heat we feel on touching a hot stove is an effect in us produced by a cause that bears no resemblance to the experience, which we know to be the mean kinetic energy of the element we touch and which Descartes would describe only as "motion" in the element. In the case of color, though, we tend to think that the color is actually in the object, even while understanding it is an effect produced in us by light and surface texture. (This point is considered in more detail in Part II.) In any case, as noted earlier, Descartes's way of structuring the nature of awareness raises a fundamental issue about whether or not we get things right in our internal representations of reality. And this issue has to do with whether or not we get things right, not only in the case of individual perceptions, but in perception generally. Descartes, therefore, faces the need to say something in general about the apparently highly problematic nature of our awareness—something he has actually stressed in developing his methodological doubt using the dream hypothesis.

To be fair to Descartes, the "representationalist" notion that awareness consists of a sort of ideational map or portrait of the world is not unique to him; he shares it with thinkers as diverse as Locke and Lenin. The problem of general error, or at least the possibility that the map or portrait may be seriously distorted, is not unique to him either. In fact, everyone following Descartes who accepts his basic representationalist view faces that same problem. But unlike most of those with whom Descartes shares the conception of awareness as possession of internal facsimiles, Descartes must reconcile the shortcomings of our perceptual and representational apparatus with a perfect Creator. Nor is it only perception that poses the problem, because obviously we err when we reason too—as the device of the evil spirit emphasizes in Descartes's methodological doubt. Error, then, once employed to generate skepticism, poses an epistemological and theological problem, because an implication of the possibility that we do not get things right in representing external reality in our minds or in reasoning is that perhaps we are *not able* to get things right. For Descartes, perception is systematically deceptive in that, even if it does not result in error, it presents such things as colors as if they were in the things themselves, when they are actually caused in us by properties of those things which are not themselves colors, such as light reflecting on specific surface textures. But this sort of *systematic* difference can be dealt with theoretically and by applying Cartesian method. The problem Descartes has, then, is that perhaps we were not created properly, and the errors we constantly make both in reasoning and perceiving are therefore ultimately God's fault for not giving us better intellectual and sensory equipment.

Descartes must block this possibility because he cannot even indirectly attribute error to God, since that would make God imperfect in that either God could not give us adequate sensory equipment, or he chose to let us fall into error, which would be to question either God's omnipotence or benevolence. Therefore Descartes must explain error in some way that does not impugn God's power or benevolence. At the same time, his methodological doubt demands that we be capable not only of being sometimes wrong, but of being systematically misled, as in the case of always conceiving colors to be in the things themselves. Descartes's solution is ingenious. He insists that God is not at fault because God gave us all the intellect and accuracy of perception we need. If we err it is our fault. Descartes explains error by recalling that since we must be free to choose between good and evil, God had to give us a perfect will. And a will's freedom cannot be qualified; a will is either free or it is not free. Since we need free will to be morally responsible for our choices and behavior, God gave us perfectly free will. However, our intellects did not have to be perfect; God gave us adequate intellects, but far from perfect ones. So when we reason or draw conclusions about our perceptions, we often err. The trouble is that our perfect wills simply outstrip our imperfect intellects.

> [E]rrors . . . depend upon two joint causes, namely, the faculty of knowing which I possess and the faculty of choice, or rather of free will—that is to say, of my understanding together with my will. For by the understanding alone I neither assert nor deny anything, but I only conceive the ideas of things which I may assert or deny. Nor in considering the understanding thus precisely can we say that any error is ever found in it. . . . Whence, then, do my errors arise? Only from the fact that the will is much more ample and far-reaching than the understanding, so that I do not restrain it within the same limits but extend it even to those things which I do not understand. (Descartes, 4:54, 56 [I:175, 176])

In short, we go around making hasty judgments. We fail to follow careful, Cartesian analytic method, and impetuously draw unwarranted conclusions and take appearances as realities and vice versa. We let our will run away with our judgment. We need not do so, but we do because we are lazy or impressionable.

It seems not to have occurred to Descartes that a perfect God could have anticipated the results of harnessing a perfect will to an imperfect intellect, and could have arranged things better. However, Descartes would argue that the possibility of error due to will overriding intellect was the price to be paid for God making us free, and that in effect the only possible better arrangement was for God to give us perfect intellects and so make us virtual gods.

But regardless of problems and objections, the point is that Descartes manages to avoid a theologically disastrous consequence of his methodological doubt and general construal of the nature of knowledge by blaming human error on hastiness of judgment.

But if error is the price of free will, there is also a high price on Descartes's ingenious solution. Notice that his solution turns on his conception of the understanding as a kind of internal arena in which ideas are present as neutral contents. That is, to have an idea is simply to attend to something which presents itself as neutral and self-contained. This means an idea is in the mind, in the understanding, the way a bill is in my pocket. As long as I do not try to spend the bill, it is "neutral," a mere presence in my pocket. It is only if I try to buy something with the bill that its authenticity becomes an issue, and it may be rejected as counterfeit. In the same way, mere awareness of the idea of a table, which seems to be before me as a material, extended object is just that, an idea present to my consciousness. It is only when I judge the idea to be of a real table, say by trying to put something on it, that I find out whether or not there is a table there and whether my idea represents a real table or fails to do so.

This "nonjudgmental" conception of the understanding as a kind of stage for ideational presentations is very odd. It requires that every perception—as opposed to a case of mere awareness—is an act of judgment. Descartes is quite explicit about this. Every step one takes along a street is preceded by a composite act of first entertaining an idea of an expanse of sidewalk and secondly judging that the idea represents a real expanse of sidewalk on which one can step. The initial absurdity of this is circumvented by claiming that with practice these assessments and judgments become extremely quick and essentially unconscious. And in case you are tempted to read this as some sort of anticipation of complex contemporary perception theory, remember that the claim here is not just that we do not apprehend things like sidewalks directly, but that every representation we experience is individually attended to as a neutral idea, considered as a possibly accurate representation of a real thing (its possible cause), and then most likely judged to be of a real thing. Everything we experience is experienced first as given, as a neutral idea, and is then judged to be a this or a that. Philosophical sophistication, then, supposedly begins with the realization that our judgments might be wrong even though they largely enable us to cope with our environment effectively. For instance, it becomes possible to think that even an extremely reliable and repeated judgment, to the effect that a certain constantly re-curring idea is a faithful representation, could turn out to be a recurring error which, for one or another reason, nonetheless has been systematically effective in prompting goal-attaining behavior.

The important point here is this: for Descartes, regardless of how well we are able to cope with what appears to us to be an objective world, it is always possible that we could learn we had been wrong all along, that what we thought were reliable percep-tions were actually just systematically lucky but erroneous ideas which related productively to our intentions and objectives. Aware-ness of the world is always inferential, so it is always possible that it is wrong. The fundamental notion is that our conscious life or experience is wholly different in kind from whatever existence we may have as material entities.

GOD AGAIN

THE fifth meditation's main point is to prove the existence of God by appealing to reason alone in the sense of using only reason as applied to the concept of God. The third meditation uses a causal argument for the existence of God, and so relies on a principle different from the concept of God itself. The proof offered in the fifth meditation purports to establish the actual existence of God by appealing only to the concept of God. Descartes borrows from the medieval philosopher and theologian Anselm of Canterbury (1033–1109) to argue that the very concept of God is such that it necessitates instantiation: that is, the concept is such that it must be the concept of an actually existent being rather than only of a possibly existent one. Recall the derivation of the concept of extension or matter. Clearly, once we have the concept of matter it is possible to think that perhaps there is no matter at all, though if there were it would be extended. The experiment with the wax only defines matter in saying what its defining characteristic would be if it existed, namely, that it would be extended. What Descartes is after now is an argument that will show that unlike the concept of matter, the concept of God by itself entails that God exists.

Do not confuse this argument, called the Ontological Argument, with the causal one. It is true that in the third meditation Descartes argues from an idea to reality, by arguing that we could only get the idea of God from something adequate to causing that idea. But that way of arguing appeals to causality, in that it appeals to how things cause other things and to how effects are supposedly never greater than their causes. However, notice that it is not self-contradictory to think that an effect might be greater than its cause. What blocks that thought is not logical inconsistency but prior acceptance of the *a priori* principle that a cause must be adequate to its effect. What Descartes wants now is an argument that allows no such possibility, where it *is* self-contradictory to understand the idea of God and think that God does not exist. And the Ontological Argument Descartes borrows from Anselm precisely holds that once we fully grasp what it is we understand when we have the idea of God, we realize that it would be self-contradictory both to think of God and to think God does not exist.

Both Descartes's and Anselm's arguments are essentially the same; there really is only one Ontological Argument, though there are slightly different versions of it. Descartes's version is perhaps the briefest. Whatever version is considered, though, one must pay close attention to the precise language used, because it is crucial to see that the argument turns on *conception* and not imagination. That is, when the argument's premises speak of understanding the concept of God, or having the concept of God, or understanding the word 'God', they mean just that. They do not mean that one understands the concept or word in the fuller sense we often use when we say someone understands something. If we say that Smith understands horses, we rarely mean that he uses the word 'horse' correctly; instead we mean he is able to work with horses, to anticipate their needs, to know what training methods work best, and so on. Many beginners confuse the notion of understanding—of conception—in the Ontological Argument with this broader sense of understanding. When Anselm and Descartes speak of understanding the concept of God or the word 'God', they mean just that; they mean no more than what one gains when one looks up the word in a dictionary.

The first presupposition leads to the second, which is that what one understands in understanding the concept of God is just that God is the perfect being, that God is "that than which no greater can be conceived." In other words, God is personified total and complete perfection. Many beginners also get confused about this, thinking that Descartes is imposing on them some particular theological conception of God. That is not the case. The only thing Descartes is imposing, following Anselm, is the idea that God is wholly perfect. If someone has a conception of God as less than perfect, whether as still in the process of becoming perfect or as lacking certain perfections, then the Ontological Argument simply fails to apply to that conception. The argument is specifically about the conception of God as the ultimate perfection, as that one Being which has every perfection or is perfect in every possible way. The argument, then, though flawed in a number of ways, does not presuppose either that we can imagine God or that God is a particular God, such as Jehovah or Allah. The Ontological Argument turns only on God's perfection, not on exhaustive understanding of God's attributes; it only requires conception or understanding of phrases like "the perfect being" or "the greatest conceivable being" or "a being lacking no perfection."

What Descartes sets out to do is establish that to understand the concept of God is to understand that God exists. The gist of the argument can be put quite briefly, though appreciating what is said requires a good bit of thought. Essentially Descartes maintains that to entertain the concept of the perfect God, and to think of God as not existent, as only an idea in the mind, is to contradict oneself. The reason is that Descartes thinks that existence is a positive property, and so a property God must have to perfection, since God must have every positive property to the ultimate degree. To think of God is to think of the Being with *every* perfection. But then, to think of God as only an idea or as nonexistent is to think of the Being with every perfection as lacking at least one perfection, namely, existence. And Descartes wants us to agree that it would be a serious imperfection in God or anything else not to be real, not to exist. Supposedly, since to think of God is to think of the Being with every perfection, to think of God is to think of God as existent, since existence is one of the perfections we attribute to God just in thinking of God as the Perfect Being. Putting things a little differently, to think of God, and to deny God's existence, is to both attribute existence to God and to deny God's existence at the same time. Anselm reminds us that this was done by the biblical fool who said "in his heart" that there is no God. Anselm's and Descartes's point is that for the fool to deny the existence of God is first to think of God, as the subject of the denial, and that is to think of a Being necessarily having existence as one of its perfections. Then it is to immediately deny existence to that Being. This is to contradict oneself as surely as if one said, "It's raining but it's not raining," and meant each phrase in the same sense and as denials of one another.

The basic problem with the Ontological Argument is that it tries to move from conception to reality, or from concepts to what they might be concepts of, in a way which allegedly traces a necessary connection. What supposedly supports that connection is the idea that existence is a property, and that as such it can be entailed or necessarily possessed by that one thing which must have every (positive) property, namely, God. Both Hume and Kant challenged the idea that existence is a property, that existence is something which a thing *has*. Hume pointed out that if I entertain the idea of a possible thing or event, I add nothing to the idea if I then think of the thing as existing or of the event as occurring or having occurred. Kant's argument is more complex and presupposes more, but its point is the same: existence is not a property, therefore it is not a perfection or a property necessarily possessed by a Being thought of as perfect. The long and short of this is that we cannot go from a concept to its instantiation purely on the basis of the concept's features.

With respect to the original formulation of the Ontological Argument, Anselm's own, one of his contemporaries, a monk named Gaunilo, argued against Anselm that if the Ontological Argument did work, it could be used to prove the existence of anything we might think of, so long as we thought of it as perfect. His example was the idea of a perfect island. However, what Gaunilo's counterarguments really bring out is that Anselm assumes far too much when he blithely asserts that we do in fact conceive or understand the idea of a perfect God. The point is quite straightforward, and does not make the mistake mentioned of confusing conception and imagination. Whether it is Anselm's or Descartes's version, the Ontological Argument would at least be more plausible if we could say more about God's perfection. But when we examine the claim that God has every perfection, we realize we really do not understand what is being claimed. Consider just two perfections which are normally attributed to God: perfect mercy and perfect justice. God supposedly is both merciful and just, and if so God must be perfectly merciful and perfectly just, since any divine attribute must be perfect. But a little thought brings out that justice is tempered by mercy and mercy requires the qualification of justice. But how can God be perfectly just and perfectly merciful if being just precisely means not being merciful and being merciful precisely means tempering justice?

However, Descartes thinks the argument proceeds without serious difficulty. He contends that he

> find[s] it manifest that we can no more separate the existence of God from his essence than we can separate from the essence of a rectilinear

triangle the fact that the size of its three angles equals two right angles, or from the idea of a mountain the idea of a valley. [I]t is no less self-contradictory to conceive of a God, a supremely perfect Being, who lacks existence—that is, who lacks some perfection—than it is to conceive of a mountain for which there is no valley. (Descartes, 5:63 [I:181])

Notice that this latter passage refers to existence being inseparable from the *essence* of God, not from the idea of God. Here we have, in fairly obvious form, the slide from idea to reality. Whether rightly or not, Descartes could have more plausibly maintained that existence cannot be separated from the idea of God. But of course that would not be enough, as it would be possible then to have the idea, complete with its necessary entailment, but God actually not exist. This is why the Ontological Argument does not prove only that when we think of God and understand the concept, we must think of God as really existing. That would not be enough. The whole point is that the necessity of God possessing all perfections, including existence, is *in the world*, not only in our ideas. That is why Descartes speaks of God's essence, not just of our idea of God. And that is why the argument is so suspect, because it seems to be a glaringly unwarranted imposition of intellectual necessity on reality.

To conclude our discussion of the Ontological Argument as offered in the fifth meditation, I will briefly raise a question that is not often asked but which deserves serious consideration, both in itself and because its discussion illustrates issues raised not by the contents of the *Meditations*, but by their structure and economy. The question is, why does Descartes offer two arguments for the existence of God? In spite of the tight discursive frugality of the *Meditations*, Descartes found it necessary to offer two different arguments for God's existence. This is an issue because, given Descartes's attempts to emulate geometric argument and proof, it seems somewhat problematic that he offer *two* proofs for God's existence. After all, provision of two arguments to the same conclusion actually tends to weaken both by suggesting that neither is sufficient. If something is a *proof*, then it needs no additional support, as might be offered by a second and independent proof. Additionally, however highly Descartes may have regarded it, the Ontological Argument had been around for a long time, and it had been challenged by many, including Thomas Aquinas, who thought the argument tainted with presumption because it seemed to require more positive knowledge of God's nature than finite beings could have. Given all he says about not relying on tradition and authority and establishing conclusions with certainty through rigorous argumentation, it does seem questionable for Descartes to include the Ontological Argument in addition to his own quite elegant causal one.

Descartes himself says little enough about his reasons for offering two arguments, but this little is suggestive. Near the end of his response to the first set of objections to his *Meditations*, Descartes tells us that "there are two ways only of proving the existence of God, one by means of the effects due to him, the other by his essence or nature, and as I gave the former explanation in the third Meditation. . . . I considered that I should not afterwards omit the other proof." (Descartes, *Reply to Objections I*, Haldane and Ross, 1969:II:22) We might note that there is some hint here of merely meeting an expectation, of including an argument which he perhaps had reservations about, because ignoring it might have seemed peculiar to his peers. My own view of Descartes's reasons, which is supported by the foregoing quotation, is that the causal argument of the third meditation, in appealing to our actual possession of the idea of God, appeals to experience, while the Ontological Argument of the fifth meditation appeals only to reason. After all, in his methodological doubt Descartes offers *two* hypotheses, the dream one and the evil spirit one, to separately impugn ideas deriving from experience and from reason. If I am right in this interpretation, the important point would be that God then emerges as the only thing capable of wholly conclusive discursive or argumentative proof on the basis of experience *and* on the basis of reason. Do not forget that the "proof" of Descartes's existence is not an *argument*; it is a direct intuition. Remember also that the proof of the existence of matter is mediated by God's goodness. God is the only thing given in experience—through the idea we have of God—which can be proven directly. But whatever Descartes's reasons for using two arguments, the point is not to pursue this issue for its own sake; rather it is to call attention to how the tight structure and economy of the *Meditations* themselves raise questions about the content. What this teaches is that philosophical arguments are assessable both with respect to what they claim and how they claim it. It must also be appreciated how the form of an argument may prompt questions about its presuppositions. However, it is time now to proceed to the final meditation.

THE WORLD, AT LAST

The sixth meditation is where Descartes fulfills his implicit promise to show that the concept of matter, which is derived in the third meditation, is instantiated: that matter or extension actually exists. The proof must wait until the sixth meditation because it is first necessary to establish both the existence of God and God's perfect nature. It is absolutely crucial to the argument of the *Meditations* that God not have need or desire to deceive. In fact, it is crucial to establish that since the need or desire to deceive is a moral imperfection, it is wholly alien to, and totally excluded by, God's essential nature.

The first thing to understand about the proof of the external world offered in the sixth meditation is that it is not, strictly speaking, a proof at all. Certainly it lacks the force of the demonstration of one's own existence. The reason is that matter can never be known directly, as can mind. Berkeley later uses this limitation to deny matter altogether, and to argue for idealism or the view that mind exhausts what there is, claiming that all things that appear to not be mind are only ideas in mind. So because extension cannot be known directly, as is made clear in the second meditation where Descartes derives the concept of extension from ideas of color and shape, there must be an inferential step in the argument for matter's existence. It is to make that step that Descartes needs God's goodness and inability to deceive. But before we proceed, a possible confusion must be discussed. Descartes is not limiting God's omnipotence by arguing that God cannot deceive us. In some sense, if God wanted to deceive us, it is within God's actual power to do so. The point is that God, being perfect, never has need to resort to deception, because God can accomplish any end through willing that it come about. The only reason God would deceive us, then, would be because God wanted to for some arbitrary reason or, like the evil spirit, for its own sake. But God is perfect, and deception is bad, so it is not in God's nature to have an arbitrary reason to deceive, much less to do so for its own sake. What appears to be a limitation, then, is supposedly only something contrary to and excluded by God's own nature. Obviously we may want to argue with this point, but what must be understood is that Descartes is not simply making a mistake by denying God deceives us.

As for the argument itself, Descartes begins by stressing the degree of conviction he feels, when he has certain ideas, that the ideas represent real things. Descartes is careful to remain within the bounds of his ideas. His conviction is that some ideas truly represent things which are not themselves ideas; he does not claim to be convinced that he senses things themselves. All of Descartes's awareness of the world is through ideas, so the issue is whether ideas truly represent things. The gist of the argument is this: Descartes notes a difference among his ideas. Some, like the idea of a unicorn, are of one sort with respect to his conviction about the nature of the idea. Others, like the idea of his own hand, are of quite a different sort. It is about the latter that he has a very firm belief that these ideas do represent real things. But what would it take for him to have that conviction and the ideas still did not represent real things? Being fooled by the evil spirit would do it, but remember that Descartes now has a sample of unquestionable truth, from the establishment of his own existence, and more significantly has proven the existence of a perfect God. The evil spirit seems to have been defeated.

Things now get tricky theologically and philosophically. There is no good reason to believe that Descartes's convictions about the representational veracity of some ideas pass the test of comparison with the self-evidence of the *cogito*. For one thing, the ideas in question are irreducibly inferential, unlike his intuition of his own existence. The conviction in question is problematic, then, as to its import. Again, there is no compelling reason to accept that even a perfect God would curtail the deceptive activities of the evil spirit. The evil spirit could be recast in the role of the religious Satan and be thought to play a continuously deceiving role and Descartes be expected by God to overcome the deception by constant doubt and argument. The likeliest reason that the evil spirit is quietly forgotten, and conviction in perceptual matters judged to be great enough that the only thing that could undermine it would be God's deception, is that a perfect God and an omnipotent evil spirit cannot coexist. So when Descartes proves the existence of a perfect God—twice over—he automatically banishes the evil spirit. What this suggests was alluded to before, namely, that in the first and second meditations the "evil spirit" is simply God under a different description, and that much of the point of the arguments for the *existence* of God has to do with the *perfection* of God and hence God's inability to deceive.

Consider now the epistemological predicament that follows from Descartes's conception of the mind and its relation to the external world. All our knowledge of the world, if there is indeed extended matter, is through the ideas we have. Our awareness of the world is always representative, that is, it is always mediated by ideas. That is why the sixth meditation's proof of the reality of extension must rely on God's veracity, and that is why the epistemological project that Descartes initiated is basically one of trying to find ways to show that our ideas are in fact faithful replicas of realities which are "external" to the mind. Given this epistemological structure, consider further that if both proofs for God's existence work, God will be the *only* thing the existence of which we can be directly certain of on the basis of possession of an idea. The existence of ideas as such is never in question, and matter's existence is something reasoned to on the basis of not only ideas but also something utterly different, namely, God's nondeceptive nature together with the conviction some of our ideas carry. And our own existence as minds is, of course, directly intuited. We have, then, only one object of knowledge with fully demonstrable reality. The reality of everything else depends on more or less justified inferences.

Supposedly, at the end of the sixth meditation, everything is as it was, except that it is now demonstrated as opposed to casually assumed. That is, Descartes's meditations have not resulted in the discernment of new information; instead, they have supposedly demonstrated the veracity of what was previously only assumed. At the end of the *Meditations* Descartes supposedly has philosophically sound reasons for accepting what he in any case believes: that he himself exists, that the world is real, that God exists. He need not fear that he is dreaming or deceived by a demon. He has shown that we are largely right in taking ourselves and the world as we take them to be. But Descartes takes his efforts to have been more than a vindication of common beliefs; he believes that in reasoning as he has, he has laid down the basic methodological principles for the future development of human knowledge.

But what Descartes actually succeeds in doing, given his assumptions and operant principles, is opening an unbridgeable gulf between consciousness and the world. What was least at issue, our own existence as thinkers, is what is best established; as for God, there was no shortage of arguments as good as or better than Descartes's; but the world has been made unreachable and distant and its reality impugned precisely by the argument that was supposed to verify it. Our belief in the reality of the world now rests precariously on the problematic goodness of a problematic God. A more critical view of where we are at the end of the *Meditations* is that Descartes, or any meditator, really knows with certainty only that thought is taking place while thought is taking place. The dream hypothesis is not really defeated, for objects of waking life are "proven" to exist only contingently on God's nondeceptiveness, and the proofs of God's existence are open to challenge. As for the demon, what is supposed to happen is that the meditator realizes that only a perfect, and so nondeceptive, God could have the powers initially attributed to the demon, so the demon should be revealed as only a skeptical device. But this result also is contingent on proving the existence of a perfect God, so Descartes seems not to have conclusively defeated the demon hypothesis either. In addition, the second, third and sixth meditations have rendered us isolated consciousnesses. We are left, then, with epistemology, namely, the hopeless project of regaining access to the world through elaborate inferential argumentation.

Before concluding this section, it may be worthwhile to comment that my foregoing remarks may appear to be unremittingly critical. Remember, though, that you must read the *Meditations* yourself, and that aside from a general sketch to guide you, it is better that Descartes speak for himself with respect to his positive theses. But in addition, you have to appreciate that the bulk of philosophy *is* critical. And learning to do philosophy is first learning to test and probe and analyze highly abstract ideas. Consider some of the more outstanding things that happen in the *Meditations*, which might otherwise be readily accepted as Descartes describes them, namely, as rigorously and soundly argued. The objective necessity of causal connection is assumed in the causal proof of God's existence in the third meditation. Descartes does not question that there is a necessary connection between a cause and an effect, as he fails to question the principle that a cause must be adequate to its effect. Later Hume was to challenge the necessity of causal connection precisely on the grounds that mere sequentiality of ideas—the way some seem to invariably follow others—does not provide a sufficient basis for arguing that the prior ones *produce* the later ones. Descartes should have anticipated Hume's critical argument, given how rigorous Descartes claims to be about philosophical doubt early in the *Meditations*. More important is that Descartes never doubts the capacity and reliability of *memory* in retaining the premises of his various arguments. Without reliable memory, Descartes could not draw his conclusions from his premises, yet there is no attempt to establish the reliability of memory, for instance against the evil spirit's efforts. Philosophical ideas are difficult, and doing original philosophy, as Descartes was doing, is more difficult still. The only way for a beginner to understand philosophical ideas, and to learn to develop them, is to examine those encountered as rigorously and thoroughly as possible. Works of philosophy are not like works of art in that they cannot be simply appreciated as presented. The reason is that philosophical ideas and theses *make claims on you* with respect to what you believe. They must, therefore, be most carefully examined. And if you still feel the foregoing exposition to be too critical, think a minute if you had begun by reading the *Meditations* before reading this text. Can you be sure you would have spotted the flaws? And do you think you would have understood Descartes's arguments as well as now that you are on guard regarding those flaws? The flaws in question are rarely of a simple sort; they involve complex and elusive presuppositions. And what would an *un*critical reading of Descartes give you? Little more than entertainment, or, more dangerously, unwarranted conviction. In any case, nothing said above precludes your deciding that Descartes was *right* and that what I have pointed out as flaws can be dealt with. The lesson can be articulated by paraphrasing Socrates: nothing unexamined is worth having.

CONCLUDING REMARKS TO PART I

Fundamental philosophical assumptions operate at so deep a level that they are seldom, if ever, reflected on except by the most perceptive of thinkers and critics. Often philosophical disputes will actually share a great deal of common ground, in sharing deep assumptions. Differences that appear major to participants in the debate often look trivial to later philosophers and historians. Deep assumptions determine the course of philosophical thinking as a riverbed determines the direction of the river's course, and it takes great effort to identify them. One of the most persistent assumptions in Cartesian thinking is the deeply rooted notion that the contents of belief and knowledge, and so the objects of epistemological philosophizing, are determinately articulable; that it is always possible to say what one believes or knows, and to do so with a critical measure of precision. This assumption is evident in Descartes in terms of the objectivity and determinateness of ideas. Descartes conceived of what he doubted, believed, or knew as determinate "presentations" to the mind, presentations having the character of objects "in" the mind. Recall that for Descartes, "objective reality" was not what it is for us, "real" reality, but rather the reality something had as an object of thought. Recall also that the arguments for the existence of God, as our best examples of this point about objective reality, rely entirely on the nature of what is present to the mind in thinking about God. If the idea of God were not determinate and specifiable, neither the causal argument of the third meditation nor the ontological argument of the fifth meditation could work, since Descartes trades on the objective reality of the idea of God—the specificity and determinateness of the idea—to establish the "formal" or actual (or "external") reality of God.

A second deeply rooted assumption in Descartes's thought is that we are capable of effective inner reflection, of objectifying our own thought processes and assessing them as we might anything else we find problematic. It is absolutely crucial to the Cartesian project that we be able to consider our ideas and the having of ideas with a measure of objectivity: that is, that we can think about thinking without altering or distorting either the objects of thought or the process of thought. Descartes proceeds as if his own internal activity of thinking and doubting were as objectively available to reflection as any series of things in our environment. Even when he imagines the evil spirit might be deceiving him, Descartes assumes that the very objectivity of his own doubting is enough to prove that the evil spirit could not be deceiving him about his own existence. For Descartes, then, the contents of knowledge and belief, of thought generally, are conveniently specific, articulable, and objective. It never occurs to Descartes that the very act of self-reflection might change the character of reflection or the objects of reflection; he never doubts the determinacy or objective reality of ideas. He thinks that the objects of his internal reflection will cooperate and remain reasonably stable so that he can proceed with his meditations and draw reliable conclusions on that basis.

To appreciate the full force of the Cartesian conception of the objects of thought as determinate and stable in reflection we can turn, not yet to Foucault, but to another contemporary. Rorty thinks that the central problem with Cartesian thinking in general, and Descartes's epistemological project in particular, is that the knowing mind is thought of as a "mirror of nature," as being what it is—conscious—by somehow reflecting a determinate reality with its ideas. (Rorty, 1979) This is precisely the Cartesian conception of awareness as a mind entertaining ideas which mirror their causes, whether God or external objects or one's own body. Given this conception, all that can be known directly are the contents of the mind itself, so it follows that the primary philosophical need is to somehow establish that the mind's representations can be faithful to their external originals. Establishing the possibility of knowledge is precisely a matter of establishing that we "get things right" in mirroring reality, that we do not distort nature in our internal representations of it. But note that the project is not one of establishing factual truths. That is, the traditional philosophical project is not the same as the scientific or empirical project. It is the latter's business to show that just this or just that idea or series of ideas conforms to reality. Cartesian philosophy concerns itself with the general possibility of achieving true knowledge.

Rorty tells us that if we have "a simple theory of the . . . mind either getting, or failing to get, a clear view of . . . [external] things," then we will naturally think that "inquiry consists in getting our 'representations' into shape, rather than simply describing the world." (Rorty, 1982:15) In addition, we will take it that what we must first do when we philosophize is not try to say how things are, but rather try to establish that we *can* know how things are by testing our ideas or internal representations against skeptical arguments such as ones about possibly dreaming or evil spirits deceiving us. Differently put, what would otherwise be taken as knowledge of the world, the content of awareness, is taken to be a complex facsimile, and so only potentially a correct portrait of reality. But since we cannot get outside of our minds to check our representations against the world, all we can do is test the possible veracity of representations against arguments that purport to show that veracity of that order can never be achieved. Descartes's dream hypothesis and evil spirit are only stand-ins for all manner of arguments that are designed to show that whatever the contents of consciousness, they may differ radically from reality.

Rorty argues that once we accept the Cartesian epistemological structure, once we accept that consciousness is essentially the having of a number of representations of external reality, then not only is Descartes's project of trying to prove those representations accurate an inevitable one, but it is also a hopeless one. The reason is that the very premise that generates the project precludes its successful conclusion. If our awareness of the world must always be indirect, through representations, we can never really know that the representations are faithful to the world. I have said much of this before, but it bears repeating because it is crucial to appreciate how the defining feature of Cartesian philosophizing is that to philosophize is primarily to test the general reliability of what are taken to be facsimiles or ideational portraits of a reality forever beyond "immediate" awareness. As has been shown, this is most evident in how the proof of the external world, of extended matter, in the sixth meditation remains an indirect one relying on God's benevolence. The world cannot be directly experienced as mind is, so there cannot be a direct intuition of it as there is of mind in the "I think, I am" of the second meditation. And for some three hundred years subsequent to Descartes, the vast majority of philosophers—the most notable exception being Hegel—took it that their main job was that of epistemological justification, of establishing through rigorous argumentation that our ideas indeed can be faithful replicas of their external causes.

There is something of a moral to be drawn from the conception of ourselves as isolated consciousnesses in touch with reality only through representations. The moral is that, as Descartes and those who followed in the tradition he established assume, truth must be autonomous and objective for there to be knowledge. The "fit" between our ideas and the world cannot be merely a matter of our perception or acceptance, for that might always be distorted or idiosyncratic. On the Cartesian scheme, knowledge can only be knowledge if the fit is guaranteed by something other than our own beliefs. There must be objective truth if there is to be knowledge at all; our ideas must conform to their causes in a way wholly independent of ourselves and that conforms to standards wholly independent of us, else we would all wind up in distinct universes where what is the case just is whatever we take to be the case. What this means is that there is how we take things to be, how things are, and the *truth* that things are as they are.

The foregoing is, in effect, a characterization of Descartes as an "objectivist," as one who believes that not only are things as they are independently, but that the truth of how they are is no one's and no time's truth. And because knowledge is possession of truth, knowledge is nonperspectival: from no particular point of view. Otherwise, it is not *knowledge*. In what follows we will consider someone who saw this idea as definitive of modern philosophy and rejected it totally. For Foucault the perspectiveless notion of knowledge is an absurdity; for him the idea that human beings might gain knowledge as a god might, from no particular point of view, is not only a dangerous myth, but also a supposed item of knowledge which is itself a result of Cartesian philosophizing and intellectual ambitions. We must now turn from the objectivist Descartes to the "constructivist" Foucault. Having begun to more fully understand a view of truth and knowledge as the autonomous and abiding objects of intellectual searching, we must begin to understand a view of knowledge and truth as the constructed products of intellectual and political activity.

PART II

FOUCAULT

THE ISSUE

UNLIKE contemporaries of Descartes and some more recent philosophers, Michel Foucault never engaged in extended polemics specifically directed against Descartes's views. Foucault worked in a milieu in which Cartesian aims, methods, and assumptions had been long since discredited, and not just in detail but in basic conception. The intellectual gap between the two philosophers was far greater than even the intervening three-hundred-odd years would explain. That gap was so broad, and we share so many of Descartes's presuppositions about knowledge and truth, that most find it very difficult to understand Foucault's radical constructivism without concentrated effort. But the holistic and drastic nature of the contrast between Descartes and Foucault is all to the good, because, following our examination of Descartes's views, our interest in Foucault's views is not in considering particular arguments against Descartes's epistemological theses, such as the direct empiricist critique of Thomas Hobbes (1588–1679) and the pragmatist critique of Peirce or the indirect phenomenological critique of Maurice Merleau-Ponty (1908–61). Our interest is not in philosophical views which still engage those of Descartes, which share some common substantive or methodological elements or even just similar problems and objectives. Instead we want to consider views which differ so radically from those of Descartes that polemical engagement is precluded. Our aim is to try to understand Descartes and Foucault not as competitors within a common intellectual arena, but as representatives of opposed and mutually exclusive extremes regarding the natures of truth and knowledge.

The sort of difference that interests us can be illustrated with the following comparison. In Aristotelian physics it was a pressing issue to explain how things in motion, such as a thrown rock, keep moving. Though the Aristotelian scheme did not include a concept of gravity as a distinct force, the basic assumption was that all things fall naturally toward the center of the Earth because, in Aristotle's geocentric world view, that was also the center of the universe, and all things were supposedly inclined to find their place there. Since gravity was not thought of as a distinct force, Aristotelian physics lacked any notion of how the Earth's attraction might be resisted or even defeated, as with speed or propulsion. Continued motion parallel to the surface of the Earth therefore required explanation. Complex aerodynamic solutions were proposed, such as one supposedly detailing how air, moving from in front of a projectile to behind it, bunched up at the rear and so kept the projectile moving for a time. But none of these were entirely convincing. The speculation and limited experimentation within Aristotelian physics did not result in a better answer to the problem. Instead, the advent of Newtonian mechanics brought about what Thomas Kuhn (1922–) calls a "paradigm shift" or a wholesale revision of fundamental perspectives, and thus of problems and proposed solutions. The Aristotelian problem about continued motion simply ceased to be a problem. In the Newtonian scheme, given gravity and inertia, what needed explaining was not why things in motion keep moving but why they stop. And as if to underscore this point, in the Newtonian scheme aerodynamics explains not why a rock keeps going for a distance when thrown, but how air resistance helps to slow and eventually stop it.

The point of the foregoing juxtaposition of radically different scientific perspectives is to show that even the great conceptual gap between Aristotle and Isaac Newton (1642–1727) was a relatively narrow one, when compared to that between Descartes and Foucault. Both Aristotle and Newton pondered the motion of objects, and though it was radically different in conception and point of departure, Newton's work would have been recognized by Aristotle as relevant to his own questions. And though he saw it as mistaken, Newton certainly understood Aristotle's work. But Descartes would have thought Foucault a madman or charlatan, and Foucault thought Descartes intellectually blinded by his history and training. In spite of likely understanding what the other was up to, neither Descartes nor Foucault would acknowledge the work of the other as legitimate. Descartes and Foucault are separated by more than a theoretical paradigm shift. Descartes pondered truth and knowledge as absolutes; Foucault pondered practices which produce notions like those of absolute truth and absolute knowledge. Descartes conceived of intellectual inquiry as an investigative activity, as a matter of learning about an objective, wholly independent reality hidden from us by ignorance, ineffective methodologies, and intellectual (largely religious) bias; Foucault conceived of intellectual inquiry as a constructive activity that manufactures a reality we take to be objective and independent and which we take to be the autonomous subject of our various investigations and resulting technologies. This is the sort of difference that interests us here, a difference in total outlook, a difference between philosophical positions which are not so much opposed to one another as exclusive of one another because each redefines the discipline within which they are positions. Positions as opposed as these do not just differ on even broad issues; they effectively constitute competing conceptions of the nature of intellectual inquiry itself.

To begin to clarify just how great the contrast is between Descartes and Foucault, note that in the previous paragraph I say that Descartes sought to investigate an objective and independent reality and that Foucault thought intellectual inquiry manufactures a reality which we take as objective and autonomous. Do not be too ready to think that Foucault's view has to do only with what we can *know*, which is how these remarks are often construed. What is likely hardest to accept in what follows is that when Foucault questions the objective nature of biological sex, and argues it is part of a complex construct, he will seem to be denying the obvious and undeniable. The easy way to make some sense of his claim is to think that he must be talking about our knowledge *as distinct from* what there *really* is. But this is just what must be avoided, for as will emerge as we proceed, the point is that *it can make no sense* to think or talk about an "objective" reality that underlies what we know, and that is what is perhaps most challenging in reading, and reading about, Foucault.

What Descartes set out to investigate was the nature of mind and, to a point, of God, as well as that of extension or matter. And he might have had to conclude, as Berkeley later would, that there really is nothing but God and mind, that there is no independent material world. But do not think that in arguing as he did, Foucault was some sort of idealist, like Berkeley but without God, who thought that human intellectual activity produces the world we then try to study. That is a *metaphysical* claim, and very much at odds with Foucault's thinking. However, it does not follow that Foucault was *not* an idealist and hence was a realist—someone who believes that reality is objective and independent of our interpretations of it. The difficulty of Foucault's position with respect to the nature of reality is that he rejects traditional philosophical categories which enable disputes such as between idealists and realists. Foucault thought our very idea of reality is a product of our thought and practice. The point here is that the categories that apply to Descartes and those who follow in his intellectual footsteps simply do not apply to Foucault, because it was precisely part of his project to speak *outside* those categories.

As suggested, the radicalness of Foucault's constructivist views is extremely difficult for most people to appreciate, let alone accept. Perhaps the briefest way to make the necessary preliminary point here is by expanding on my above remark about the likeliest misinterpretation of Foucault's constructivist views on sexuality. It is tempting to read *The History of Sexuality* as if it were about how we construe a series of biological facts; as if it were about how we interpret the "given" that is sex. Many read *The History of Sexuality* as if it were about what we usually consider as *gender*, and as leaving untouched the underlying reality of sex. But Foucault's project is precisely to show how the notion of objective biological sex is *itself* a construct. This is a very hard idea to assimilate. Consider this comparison: someone claims that Aristotelian and Newtonian physics were two competing ways of construing the physical reality of the world which is itself independent of how it is variously construed. Someone else claims that *it makes no sense* to speak of an "independent" reality, because *there is no difference* between a reality that is accessible in its objective state only from a God's-eye point of view—that is, from *no* point of view—and one that simply does not exist. However hard one may find some of Descartes claims, this is harder: that the most basic idea we have, of a reality "out there" indifferent to our interpretations of it, is a product of our own thought and history. And what is harder still is that in denying the coherency of postulating a "brute" reality beyond our interpretations, one is not denying reality. The reason is that it makes no more sense to *deny* an objective reality than it does to *affirm* its existence. The point is that the very idea of such a reality is a product of doing the kind of philosophy Descartes did.

Charges of metaphysical denial of objective reality, charges of nonrealism or idealism against Foucault by traditionally inclined philosophers, are an excellent example of how insufficiently careful reading and assessment allow assumptions and expectations to color our understanding of philosophical claims and theses. Part of what made Foucault a postmodern is that he saw through what Descartes saw as pressing issues about realism and challenges to it. Foucault saw beyond epistemological puzzles generated by dubious distinctions and realized that whatever we might say about the world, *everything* we say—and think and do—is interpretive. Foucault saw that it is therefore philosophically primitive to focus on impossible questions about how things are in their supposed uninterpreted, "real" state, how they look from no particular point of view, outside any particular belief-context, and that is just what Cartesian epistemology did and does. In suggesting that Foucault was some sort of metaphysical nonrealist or idealist, in worrying whether he somehow denied brute reality in rejecting the traditional conceptions of truth and knowledge and making the claims he made about truth's and knowledge's natures, values and roles, then, we wrongly impose on Foucault just those categories and distinctions which he most questioned and which he enabled us to get beyond.

Having called attention to the danger of misunderstanding Foucault's transcendence of Cartesian epistemology as some sort of nonrealism or idealism, it seems natural to go on to say that one should also be cautious about more positive interpretations of Foucault. Rorty has noted that "the American Foucault is Foucault with most of the Nietzscheanism drained away" and that the "French Foucault is the fully Nietzschean one." (Rorty, 1991:193) And between these conservative and radical extremes there are numerous other positions. Foucault's popularity is such that there are many interpretations of his work, most differing only in degree or emphasis, but some differing in quite drastic ways. Foucault's work invites broadly divergent interpretations, and it does so not only because of its complexity but also because its most mature presentation was precluded by Foucault's early death. One should not too readily accept one or another interpretation as adequate, and certainly not as definitive. Happily, for our purposes it is not necessary to attempt to offer anything like a definitive characterization of Foucault's work; we want only to sketch enough of its "genealogical" constructivist core to provide the sharpest contrast to the objectivist epistemology of Descartes.

To continue, the best way to start our consideration of Foucault's postmodern position is by saying a little about truth, since the nature of truth is most particularly at issue between Descartes and Foucault and determines their respective views on knowledge.

The way that truth or being true usually gets explained is in terms of a relation between a descriptive sentence (or thought or judgment) on the one hand, and a "fact" on the other. If there is a cup on a table, and we choose to say so in order to offer an example of a true sentence, we are inclined to say that what makes the sentence 'The cup is on the table' true, is the cup's being on the table or the fact that the cup is on the table. The relation the sentence is thought to bear to the fact has been called one of "correspondence." That is, the sentence 'There is a cup on the table' is described as true because the sentence corresponds, or is in the relation of correspondence, to the cup's actually being on the table. We say that a sentence (spoken or written or thought) is true when it corresponds to what is the case, what is actually so.

Some have gone so far as to argue that the various grammatical elements of sentences, such as the noun 'cup', correspond individually to elements of facts or actualities, like the actual cup, and that the grammatical relationships among substantives and predicates in sentences replicate the relationships among objects like the cup and the table. The truth of a sentence, then, is taken to be accurate replication of a fact by a set of words in a certain configuration. The classic statement of this view, in the early work of Ludwig Wittgenstein (1889–1951), is usually called the "picture-theory" of meaning because it essentially held that a sentence has meaning and is true by being a linguistic picture of a fact in virtue of the arrangement of its elements. The parallel is to how the different colored areas of a photographic image comprise a picture of whatever was photographed. The picture-theory of meaning, then, was thought to spell out how it is that sentences mean what they do by corresponding (or failing to correspond) to facts, and so how they manage to sometimes be true. (Wittgenstein supposedly got the idea of linguistic replication when he saw model cars used to represent an accident and thought to himself: "That is a proposition!")

But while Wittgenstein's picture-theory is a highly technical formulation of correspondism, the conception of truth as correspondence is very widespread and seems so natural to most people that they have trouble understanding, first, that the correspondence theory of truth is a theory, and second, that there might be alternatives to it. Nonetheless, while the correspondence view may seem natural and sounds reasonable enough when articulated, it loses its persuasiveness when we begin to wonder how words, however arranged, manage to "hook up" to events or distributed objects in order to make sentences linguistic replicas of them. That is, we begin to wonder just how helpful the picturing idea is in trying to understand correspondence when we realize that both notions are metaphorical and too much alike for one to explain the other. We then begin to doubt that the notion of correspondence explains anything at all. It is also mysterious just how we might go about telling that some relation of correspondence holds between a sentence and a fact, since we cannot get outside of our language and our beliefs to compare what we say or think with how things are independently of what we say and think.

The foregoing are the sorts of questions which drove many to endorse the main rival to the correspondence theory, namely, the coherence theory of truth. In this latter theory, to say of a sentence that it is true is not to say anything about its relation to the world; rather it is to say something about its relation to other sentences. Specifically, it is to say that a sentence coheres or fits with other sentences taken to comprise an accepted set or subset of sentences. To say a sentence is false is to say it fails to cohere or does not fit with the standard set or subset. We might express the central point, in the briefest possible way, by saying that while correspondence is an extralinguistic relation (from language to something outside language), coherence is an intralinguistic one (from one part of language to another). However, the coherence theory is, because of its unfamiliarity and its nonrealist implications, an elusive and difficult theory. Suffice it to say at this point that what is crucial for us is that the correspondence theory explains truth in terms of the relations sentences supposedly bear to the world or parts of the world, while the coherence theory explains truth in terms of the relations sentences bear to other sentences.

To clarify how the Cartesian and Foucauldian views on truth differ, I must say a bit more about Descartes; in particular, I have to say how his was a correspondist view of truth and how his view shaped later epistemology. If Descartes had not tried to establish the existence of God and of the world, he would have limited himself to a kind of coherence theory of truth more or less by default, because he would have been able to relate his ideas only to other ideas. But given his attempted proofs of God's and the world's existence, he becomes a correspondist in so far as he tries to relate his ideas of God and extended stuff to external things, namely, God and the material world. Moreover, as was noted at the close of Part I, Descartes must eschew the coherence theory or conception of truth because, given how he isolates each consciousness, without correspondence every mind's reality would be individual and peculiar to that mind.

The shift in the foregoing paragraphs from sentences to ideas highlights the fact that Descartes's correspondist view of truth was more simply conceived than contemporary theories. Correspondence for Descartes was between ideas and their causes or sources, rather than between sentences and facts. Or to put it in his own terms, correspondence was between the "objective reality" of ideas and the "formal reality" of their subjects. The causal argument for the existence of God turns precisely on the notion that the objective or ideational reality of the idea of God is so great that its correspondence to the formal reality of God is obvious because only that formal reality could have produced the objective reality of the idea.

For Descartes, then, ideational replication was not actualized in asserted sentences (or propositions) corresponding to what they described, but rather in entertained and assented-to ideas imaging their causes: "ideas in me are like paintings or pictures, which can . . . fall short of the . . . original from which they have been drawn. . . ." (Descartes, 3:40 [I:163]) But there is some ambiguity here due to Descartes sometimes speaking of ideas as *acts* of the mind, in spite of seeming to have more often thought of them as like images attended to. Descartes himself comments on this: "in this word 'idea' there is an equivocation. For it can either be taken . . . as an operation of my intellect . . . or it can be taken objectively for the body which is represented by this operation. . . ." (Do not forget Descartes's special sense of "objective" as relating to the reality of ideas as ideas. Descartes, *Meditations* Preface:10 [I:138])

Causality is also a complicating factor in whatever we may say about Cartesian ideas and truth as correspondence. In a 1644 letter to Mesland, Descartes specifically says that he considers "the difference between the soul and its ideas as the same as that between a piece of wax and the . . . shapes it can take." (Kenny, 1970:148) Ideas are like imprints or forms taken by the mind, some of which are of external things and so are effects in a way that linguistic constructions are not. Imprints or assumed forms may do or fail to do justice to their causes, by being accurate replicas or blurred or otherwise distorted. But the way sentences may or may not do justice to what they describe has to do with what we choose to say, not just with causes acting on us and making us think and say certain things. There is a discrepancy, then, between how ideas may be true or false and how sentences may be true or false. And it seems whatever we might say about sentences, what are primarily true or false for Descartes are ideas conceived of as mental representations.

In the Cartesian scheme the parallel between a knowing mind and a camera is almost exact. 'Camera' derives from the Latin for 'room' or 'enclosure', and Descartes's conception of mind is that of an enclosure containing ideas, as a camera and its film contain images. The significance of this is that if there is to be knowledge of anything other than the mind's own contents, it must be in virtue of the truth of internal representations; in virtue of some of those contents being caused by and accurately representing things outside the mind. And the only applicable notion of such representation is that of accurate replication or portrayal.

What is significant about the foregoing in the present context is that for Descartes knowledge could not be only interpretation of the world in the sense of the mind's contents only bearing an approximate or even merely functional resemblance to their external causes. Anything short of faithful portrayal would be not only inexact but deceptive, and so could not be knowledge. But having said this, we must immediately qualify it. In spite of the fact that I have spoken of ideas replicating their subjects, Descartes—as will emerge in a moment—did not believe that ideas are in every respect exact copies of those subjects insofar as those subjects are the causes of ideas. Descartes's qualifications have to do with theoretical considerations about the nature of extended objects and their characteristics and what the senses can apprehend and what the mind can know. Nonetheless, the fact remains that in general, the basic assumption is that for there to be knowledge, our ideas must conform adequately to the things in the world. What underlies this assumption goes all the way back to Plato, and is the notion that anything less than cognition of eternal verities amounts only to "opinion," not knowledge. That is why, for Plato, there could not be knowledge of empirical matters, for they are by nature changing.

In spite of having taken his cue from Plato, Descartes thinks that God's surety suffices to guarantee that we can have knowledge of the empirical world. However, as just noted above, Descartes has qualifications to make about replication. In fact, the notion of ideational replication is possibly not even coherent, because while representational Cartesian ideas in the mind can only be effects of external objects, they cannot exactly resemble their causes. We understand how colors, for instance, are products of complex interactions of light and surfaces and events in the retina and optic nerve. Colors are not in the objects as such; they are produced by the objects' textures, reflected light, and so on. Even Plato recognized that our senses involve causal processes and that the end results cannot be precisely the same as their causes. In the *Theaetetus* Plato offers an intricate causal account of perception in which colors are products of various interactive "motions." The account is not one we would now take seriously, but it is nonetheless a theoretical one of the right sort. (Cornford, 1957:45–60) Descartes is also too sophisticated to believe that colors and other qualities are objective features of material things. He himself tells us that "although everyone is commonly convinced that . . . ideas . . . are wholly similar to the objects from which they proceed . . . I cannot see any reason which assures us that this is so." And further, experienced qualities "can be explained without the need to suppose anything in their matter other than . . . motion, size, shape, and arrangement of . . . parts." (Descartes, *The World*, Cottingham, 1985:81, 89) Additionally, Descartes maintains that "in order to have sensory perceptions the soul does not need to contemplate any images resembling the things which it perceives." (Descartes, *Optics*, Cottingham, 1985:166) There is a serious ambiguity, then, in the notion of adequate replication. Somehow ideas may be faithful image-like portraits of external realities, but without being exact replicas. It is difficult, therefore, to know precisely what it is that God guarantees with respect to the veracity of our ideas.

Nor is the problem one of replication only. Descartes tells us that he has "two completely different ideas of the sun: the one has its origin in the senses . . . the other is derived from astronomical considerations. . . ." (Descartes, 3:38 [I:161]) The distinction here is between what is experienced as existing and what is theoretically understood to exist, so clearly there can be two representational ideas which differ in kind but are somehow of the same thing. In a nearly contemporary instance of this distinction, Sir Arthur Eddington (1882–1944) made much of the difference between a wooden plank as seen by a layperson and as conceived by a physicist, namely, a plank experienced as a solid object and known to be a cloud of atoms in mostly empty space. (Overstreet, 1931:55) We might well ask which of these sorts of ideas is underwritten as representing real things by the guarantee of existence in the sixth meditation.

However, the foregoing is too complex to pursue further in a brief introductory book. My purpose in considering this issue about the qualification to replication is only to alert the reader to the sort of issue that can arise and to call attention to the complexity of the apparently straightforward claim that we have knowledge of the world in virtue of possessing ideational replicas of that world. And what is most notable in all this is that at base Descartes and contemporary correspondists are of a mind on one essential point: knowledge of the world has to do with the replicative accuracy of something in the mind (or which issues from the mind in speech) with respect to something outside the mind. Nor does this apply only to *a posteriori* or empirical truths about the world. If there is truth of a purely *a priori* sort, the sort which only the evil genius can impugn, it could not be a function of a correspondence internal to thought, i.e., a relation among thoughts or propositions. A thought or proposition which is true *a priori* must correspond to an objective eternal truth. Cartesian correspondism, then, requires some sort of Platonic realm of absolute truth which contains what *a priori* truths correspond to.

These remarks about truth, truncated though they may be, bring out that for Descartes and the tradition he initiated, our only access to the world is through ideas which represent the external world, and that those ideas are then true only when they are accurate portraits. What is important for us is that the essential thought was the same for Descartes as for contemporary correspondists with respect to truth: an idea is true if it corresponds to what it is an idea of; a sentence is true if it corresponds to the fact it states. The key point here is that whether it is an idea or a belief, whether or not articulated in language, or the sentence that articulates the idea or belief, whatever is judged to be true is something which faithfully captures or reproduces what is outside the mind. To be a knowing subject, then, is to have accurate internal representations of the external world. And if this is so, the core of philosophy must be epistemology, since it is precisely epistemology's job to justify the accuracy of our internal representations of the world.

The fatal flaw in the foregoing conception is that because all we can ever know directly are ideas, since we cannot get past our ideas to the reality they represent, the epistemological project must be ultimately hopeless. Regardless of how rigorous our epistemological arguments may be, the simple fact is that the Cartesian epistemological question—how we can know our ideas faithfully represent reality—is unanswerable because the Cartesian conception of knowledge limits direct knowledge to ideas. In other words, the problem has been set up in a way that precludes its ever being solved. At best we might attain inferential knowledge that our alleged internal mirrorings accurately reflect reality. But that is really not enough, for so long as such knowledge is inferential, it fails to meet Descartes's own extremely strict requirement for foundational knowledge, namely, that it precisely *not* be inferential and be immediate and direct. Descartes's quest for certainty leads only to an epistemological impasse generated by his own stipulated conditions.

It should now be somewhat clearer how conceptions of knowledge determine those of truth, and vice versa. For the Cartesian correspondist, to have knowledge is to have true representations, and for those representations to be true is for them to correspond to or faithfully portray their subjects. On the other hand, if we begin with the conception of truth as accurate portrayal of, or correspondence to, things and events, then to have knowledge must be to possess some of these accurate ideational portraits or items which somehow structurally correspond to how things are. Either conception leads to the same impasse: if we cannot have direct access to anything except our own ideas, our main problem must be the basic epistemological one of how to tell when we have accurate ideational portraits or when our thoughts or sentences correspond to reality. But the conditions that raise the problem also insure that it is insoluble, so long as those same conditions continue to determine the conception of knowledge.

THE ALTERNATIVE

THE Cartesian epistemological im-
passe, which has haunted philosophy since Plato and dominated
the discipline since Descartes, prompts some contemporaries to
argue that the Cartesian view of the human mind as an ideational
mirror of nature is hopelessly confused and produces only insur-
mountable epistemological problems. (Rorty, 1979; 1982; 1991)
And the charge is not just that Descartes got it wrong. There is no
implication that there is a *right* way of framing, and so of answering,
his questions about knowledge. The charge is that what Descartes
did or tried to do is radically misconceived in its entirety.

Though, as said above, Foucault did not address Descartes's
work specifically, he did renounce the Cartesian tradition, and the
heart of Foucault's position, and of the postmodern critique of
epistemology generally, is that there are no absolutes, that absolute
truth and knowledge are products of interpretive and theoretical
practices which are themselves products of particular histories. Descartes's project, then, is something needing explanation, not com-
pletion. There is no method by which we can acquire truth and
establish that what we take to be knowledge truly is awareness of
how things are, independently of how we think they are. To hold
knowledge hostage to development of such a method is to disallow
knowledge.

Crucial to the postmodern critique of traditional philosophy is
the view that if history had been different, for instance if Descartes

had not thought and written as he did, we would not now face the epistemological problems we face, because we would not conceive of truth and knowledge as we now do and there would be no felt need to establish the veracity of internal representations. More than that, we would not think of awareness of the world as possession of so many problematic representations. A different history would have resulted in different problems and different conceptions. Critics of the Cartesian conception of philosophy find no inevitability in the development of intellectual history; they do not believe that Descartes merely articulated what someone would have eventually realized or discovered. For them there are no philosophical truths which are like undiscovered continents that inevitably must be found. In fact, as was suggested at the beginning of Part II, for them not even scientific truths are discovered; even these are things we partly manufacture through our interests and discourses.

Foucault, perhaps the foremost Continental postmodern thinker, thought that knowledge is a product of complex cognitive factors interacting with equally complex historical factors, and not information read off the face of nature. And while Foucault thought Descartes and his followers were deeply wrong in conceiving of knowledge as they did, he also thought Descartes was at least as wrong in thinking of the knowing subject as an autonomous consciousness somehow above and beyond the ideas that consciousness entertains and the world those ideas might represent. Foucault once spoke of wanting to "cleanse" history of "transcendental narcissism." (Foucault, 1972:203) What he meant was that we have to reject not only the notion of knowledge as mirroring nature, but also the notion of ourselves as dimensionless points of consciousness somehow beyond a material world which we know only indirectly. According to Foucault, we must understand that we are not autonomous subjects defined by an intrinsic nature, subjects that passively entertain ideas which may or may not represent inaccessible objects of (inferential) knowledge. Foucault believed that we are subjects only insofar as we are shaped and molded as subjects by the events that comprise our personal histories. Just as he believed that the world, as the object of our awareness, is a manufactured object of knowledges (note the plural) produced by our discourses and practices, he thought that we, as reflective subjects, are the products of those same discourses and practices. And as noted earlier, what is most difficult about these views is surmounting the tendency to think that Foucault must be excluding the most basic facts or the brute reality of such things as that unsupported things fall because of gravity and that sex is as real as anatomical differences between men and women. And still more difficult is the idea that something as fundamental as our very being as subjects—that which Descartes precisely found most evident and unquestionable—is itself also a *result* of history, of discourse and of practice. Descartes's project of using principle-governed reasoning to discover fundamental objective truths was at the heart of modern thought and has dictated the conceptions of truth and knowledge since then. It is all the harder, therefore, to understand that for Foucault truths and knowledge are products of practices, of relations of power, of preferred discourses, and of history. What must be grasped is the claim that rather than being accurate representations, truths are the fruits of the technologies we produce to cope with the world, and knowledges (again, note the plural) are accepted networks of interrelated truths. Moreover, changes in truth or knowledge are not due to discovery of error and so of more profound truth, and hence acquisition of more complete knowledge. Any changes are due to the abandonment of some practices in favor of others, adoption of new discourses and vocabularies and rejection of old ones, and consequent reconstruals of history. In Foucault's project, then, we find the polar opposite to Descartes's quest for absolute truth and timeless knowledge. The only quest possible for Foucault is tracing how construals of subjects came to be, first, construals, and, second, accepted *as* knowledge or possession of truth.

At this point I need to make a terminological clarification. Foucault's concept of power-relations is a difficult one, and it is made more difficult by his often casual use of terms. Too often Foucault himself and commentators on Foucault speak of "power" without making it clear that Foucault's notion is not of something quite so readily denoted and certainly not of something so apparently substantive. Foucault himself, in an interview near the end of his life, said "I hardly ever use the word 'power' and if I do . . . it is always a short cut to the expression . . . relationships of power." (Bernauer and Rasmussen, 1988:11) A quick look at his works shows the overly optimistic nature of this remark, for he constantly uses the term "power" on its own. However, we must take him at his word that what he means on these many occasions is to speak of power-relations. Power-relations are dynamic and changing, and of very diverse kinds; 'power' is too static and specific a term to denote what concerns Foucault. In what follows I sometimes use the phrase 'power-relations' and sometimes the term 'power', but what determines which is used has to do either with contrasting Foucault's notion with the traditional one or with the desire for brevity. When it is Foucault's notion of power that is in question, reference is always to a hugely complex system of relations and not to something like a singular force.

Before saying more about Foucault's project, it is necessary to caution against a likely and serious confusion. Many dismiss Foucault's abandonment of a Cartesian conception of truth in favor of truth conceived as always relative to some group's or culture's or even an individual's standard as "mere relativism," as if anything like a relativistic view were simply not worth taking seriously. But additionally, they erroneously think that Foucault is offering an alternative *in kind*. What is missed in this simplistic reading of a difficult position is that Foucault is not offering a theory of truth; he is maintaining that truth is political, not just that it is relative in nature as opposed to absolute. In other words, Foucault is not offering a philosophical theory of truth at all, not if "philosophical theory" means a theory falling within traditional definitional limits. To think that he is—or must be—doing so is to insist on imposing on Foucault precisely the standards and methods he rejects in renouncing modern or Cartesian philosophizing. A large part of the point of Foucault's postmodern position is that he denies the very possibility of theorizing about the nature of truth at all. His objective is more a matter of *replacing* the traditional philosophical notion of truth with the notion of power-relations. It bears reiterating that the contrast between Descartes and Foucault is total. However mind-stretching it may be to understand Foucault's radically different claims when one's intellectual background is essentially Cartesian, customary conventional thinking must not be allowed to obscure the revolutionary import of Foucault's claims.

But it would be as simplistic and as wrong to then think that Foucault is offering a theory of something called Power:

> there is no Power, [only] power relationships which are being born incessantly, as both effect and condition of other processes. If mine were an ontological conception of power, there would be, on one side, Power with a capital P . . . and on the other side, the resistance of [those] obligated to bow before power. I believe an analysis of this kind to be completely false, because power is born out of a plurality of relationships. [P]ower is nothing other than . . . the form, differing from time to time, of a series of clashes . . . of the political, economic type, etc. Power . . . is something like the stratification, the institutionalization, the definition of tactics. . . . (Foucault, 1989:187–88)

Foucault's is not simply a philosophical view opposed to that of Descartes. As I have stressed, the choice of Descartes and Foucault for consideration in this book had to do with the fact that they are precisely not adversaries merely in the sense of holding opposed positions. As illustrated in my comparison of Aristotle and Newton, the point is that Descartes and Foucault each conceives of intellectual inquiry so differently from the other that they cannot be intellectual adversaries in anything like the usual sense. What they offer is not competing positions on the same topics but alternative world views. For Descartes truth was sacrosanct, and had to be the objective of every intellectual quest, because truth was how the world is, and so knowledge could only be cognitive reflection of that reality. For Foucault "truth" is almost incidental, it is merely that which happens to reign at a particular time and as a function of a particular set of power-relations, and knowledge is just what we call having (read: believing) this local and temporary truth. We might make the comparison in this way: for Descartes, truth was autonomous and the all-encompassing prize of inquiry, and knowledge was possession of that prize; for Foucault truth is only symptomatic of underlying structures of power-relations and history, and the prize of inquiry is understanding the structures that support what are judged to be truth and knowledge.

We have to proceed by amplifying an earlier caution about the difficulty of understanding how radical Foucault's thought was. One must guard against slipping into thinking, as many do, that what Foucault is writing about in *The History of Sexuality* is sexuality or gender as distinguished from sex. Foucault is not only showing where and how we got our present construal of sex and our sexual practices; he is concerned to show how what we take to be sexuality evolved as a social construct and subject matter and came to be taken as the reality of human sexual nature. But that does *not* mean that he differentiates between sexuality and an underlying, objective biological matter of fact, namely, sex. Foucault contends that "it is precisely this idea of sex *in itself* that we cannot accept without examination." He goes on to ask "[i]s 'sex' really the anchorage point that supports the manifestations of sexuality, or is it rather a complex idea that was formed inside the deployment of sexuality?" (Foucault, 1980:152) Later Foucault tells us that "the deployment of sexuality . . . was what established this notion [of objective] 'sex'." In short, rather than taking sexuality to presuppose sex, Foucault is arguing that our notion of sex derives from our conception of sexuality.

At this point it may seem difficult, as was anticipated above, to know what we are to make of undeniable and evident anatomical and biological realities in the face of the claim that sex is not objective, not a "given," and that it is a construct. The first thing to do here is to recall the point made earlier, and to ask what difference there could be between a brute reality that is accessible only from a God's-eye point of view and one that does not exist at all. The point of this largely rhetorical question is that it can make *no sense* to talk about or even to postulate the brute reality of sex if we can only think and talk about sex in and through our conceptions and construals. All we succeed in doing if we try to do so is precisely to create a notion of an objective but inaccessible reality. And what most worries Foucault in this connection is that we then use that created reality to justify our practices. When you read *The History of Sexuality* and what follows, you must guard against reading "sexuality" as denoting something distinct from sex, something that only supervenes on a biological reality. If you think this point has been made abundantly clear and is here needlessly repeated, consider that, as will emerge, it is precisely Foucault's message that discourse determines conception. The need for reiteration is that a point may be blunted by being too readily accepted in the abstract, and needs to be emphasized to maintain acute awareness of its force and implications. And if you are puzzled by what seems to be a denial of the obvious, you must persevere and read what follows in a consciously open-minded way, which means that whenever you are tempted to dismiss something as unacceptable or absurd, it is just then that you must work hardest at appreciating the point.

Even though it is the aim of *The History of Sexuality*, Foucault's most fundamental concern is not to expose what he describes as the myth that our culture has repressed sexuality since at least the Victorian era. Foucault has a broader agenda, and his overriding concern is to use the development of sexuality to show how a particular construal of something comes to constitute knowledge. Foucault's basic tactic, as exemplified by *The History of Sexuality*, is to provide a competing narrative-account of an institution's or phenomenon's history by highlighting the marginal and unusual, by drawing attention to the underemphasized and the ignored, and so constructing a historical sequence with different dominant features and direction. Consider the following very simple example, which may be of use in beginning to clarify the nature of Foucault's narrational reconstruals. Imagine that someone has produced a report on a relatively new nation, detailing the armed struggles

leading to its creation and in which it has engaged since, and drawing the conclusion that the nation in question has a warlike culture.
The objective of the report might be political, say to restrict arms
sales to the nation in question, or it may be more academic. In
either case, a politically delineated group of people and an emerg-
ing culture are characterized in a particular and negative way on
the basis of a series of documented conflicts. Notice that on a Cartesian interpretation, the characterization of the subject nation as
warlike is right or wrong. This sort of characterization is quite
complex, so it would be necessary to include numerous qualifications, but generally our example's report would be judged either
to capture the essential nature of the subject nation's short history
or not. Success or failure would be attributed to the thoroughness
and perceptiveness of the research and the perspicacity of the
report's conclusions, or to error, incomplete information, or
distortion.

Suppose now that we take a Foucauldian approach to the issue
of the subject nation's warlike character. We might begin our work
by noting that the researcher compared the subject nation's history
to that of other, longer-lived nations in her research and preparation of the report. We might also note that she deemed something
to be an armed conflict merely if military forces were alerted and
a number of lives lost. Our alternative basis for comparing the
subject nation's history to others might be quite different. For instance, we might work out compensatory comparative devices to
adjust for the relative ages of the nations compared. We also might
look closely at the subject nation's practices and note that its military
is often relied on to deal with national emergencies, such as floods
and earthquakes, which would mean that military alerts, even when
paired with loss of life, do not necessarily identify conflicts with
other nations. These are the obvious sorts of things we might do.
But we might next look not at the subject nation but at the researcher's own nation and culture, and trace certain traditions in
its political and academic institutions. For example, we might find
that culture's own warlike character evident in its ready construal
of all international disputes as actual or potential armed conflicts.
We might also find a national interest in making the subject nation
appear warlike. We can readily imagine researchers, though quite
innocent of Foucault's work, employing some of his techniques and
exposing the vested interests present in our example's report,
thereby revealing as self-serving the characterization of the subject
nation.

The point of the example is that nothing need be disputed regarding the basic events detailed in the researcher's report, such as the military being alerted and lives being lost. The same data can be made to tell a different story when differently organized and presented. The same data that support the warlike characterization might provide reason to say that relatively few conflicts occurred over the span of time that the subject nation has been in existence, and that rather than being warlike, the subject nation makes enlightened use of its arguably necessary defense forces. Or we might use the actual data collected, contrasting it with data not gathered, to force perception of the researcher's own culture and nation as inclined to be warlike or as diplomatically manipulative, perhaps further showing that, in comparison, the nation discussed by the report is peace loving and restrained in its use of force.

The example here is a very simple one that does little more than illustrate the important point which, once made, seems obvious: data can support various interpretations and as many different conclusions, some of which may be diametrically opposed to others. This simple example illustrates that interpretations are underdetermined by data. That is, data never of themselves impose a particular interpretation. What is crucial are the interests which motivate the attention we pay to something. Those interests not only influence interpretation, they initially determine how a report such as the one in our example comes to be thought needed and then prepared. On present construals of the nature of nations, the activities of nations as such are fairly limited. Nations engage in trade, they compete among themselves for the loyalties or cooperation of other nations, and for scarce resources. But the most notable activity of nations, because of the significance of the immediate consequences, is warring with other nations. As soon as we start thinking of nations, therefore, we have an experience-based inclination to think of conflicts; we are disposed to focus on wars and their frequency when we consider nations in various contexts. Reports such as the one we are considering do not occur to their authors for no reason; they arise from particular interests. And these interests and concerns have histories: they are themselves products. What they are products of are broad attitudes and concerns which characterize the always problematic relations among nations existing in a world of limited resources. It is therefore all but inevitable that interest in a given nation will be of a certain sort and call for certain sorts of information. When we objectify a nation, when we make it a subject of study, then, we will do so in a certain way. However, it may be very important to call attention to what may go unnoticed, given currently operant attitudes and concerns, namely, the lack of conflict during longish periods of time or imaginative and productive peaceful uses of the military. Periods during which a nation is at peace tend to go unnoticed precisely because they usually involve nothing that calls our predisposed attention to them, and uses of the military may always appear aggressive, given standard expectations and perceptions. Military activity and conflict are presently the most salient features of nations as a subject matter. In order to better appreciate the sort of interests that govern the conception and preparation of the report in our example, then, we should focus not on the salient but on the obscure and the obscured. And when we do so, we will realize that the salient is not salient because it is *in itself* what is most dominant and important, but rather is salient because of our expectations and interests.

The foregoing may be clear enough, but it is necessary to introduce further complications if we are to get a handle on Foucault's procedure and position. Notice that in our example the data regarding the subject nation's armed conflicts has not been questioned. What has been raised is the possibility that it may support widely varying interpretations. It might be assumed, then, that the matter has to do only with interpretation, that the raw data are clear enough: there were a number of military alerts, which were adequately recorded if not always adequately described or explained. The only question then seems to be what we are to make of them. Most will think that while what we do with the data may be problematic, we have no reason to seriously question the data unless there is evidence of erroneous compilation or falsification. But consider this: what counts as an alert? Even if we narrow the category of military alerts to armed conflicts, the problem remains. We must consider whether the data at issue lump offensive wars and defensive responses to invasion as all "armed conflicts." And there are more subtle points. Do the data count two conflicts as distinct even though it is arguable that one was a continuation of the other after a period of inactivity or even a negotiated ceasefire? If so, the conflict-count includes too much. On the other hand, do the data count several conflicts as an ongoing war even though the time separating them was considerable and the issues fought over were arguably different? If so, the conflict-count includes too little. What of expeditionary actions conducted at the request of another nation? And how extensive must conflicts be to count? Does a raid by a small group of commandos count? What of the actions of a single soldier? What about the actions of someone who is not a uniformed soldier, such as a spy or agent provocateur? Will we count an armed conflict if it is entirely internal, as in the case of a riot or a civil war? And there are other complications: consider that we or the subject nation may not count something as a conflict at all if it is properly sanctioned, as in the case of military suppression of insurrection. If none of the earlier questions suffice to shake confidence in the objectivity of data, this last point should make evident that what counts as a conflict in our example is a political issue, not a factual one. We all know too well how something may be legitimate suppression of insurrection to some, and outrageous crushing of justified protest to others.

Foucault insists that the data supporting varying interpretations and conclusions are themselves products of interpretation. Interpretation goes "all the way down"; there simply is no bedrock that is both free of interpretation and value-neutral and that supports more obviously interpretive and value-laden conclusions. Interpretation conditions and shapes not only what we conclude from evidence, but what sort of thing or event we deem to *be* evidence and how particular things and events are taken as being evidence. Intellectual inquiry, then, is not Cartesian discovery but discernment of operant influences which shape and determine whatever has come to be the subject matter of inquiry, a subject matter which itself comes to be objectified as a topic by those same or similar influences.

As is clear in *The History of Sexuality*, as well as in *Discipline and Punish*, Foucault engages in meticulous tracing and relating of quite elusive factors in order to put together his alternative histories and to make manifest the interests that shape what are then taken as objective events. And this is where we encounter what many see as the most serious ambiguity in Foucault's work, one made evident by how his critics focus most intensely on his historical claims. The problem is that Foucault appears to proceed as if unearthing little-known facts, though he is, by his own principles, offering a retrospective reinterpretation. He cannot be claiming to have discovered heretofore ignored or obscured truths. *The History of Sexuality* may look to the naive reader like a historical exposé, like a more accurate interpretation, one contrary to the accepted interpretation but nonetheless of actual developments. However, this reading is at odds with Foucault's most basic claim, that it is relations of power that make something a development, and that different relations result in different contemporary developments and different interpretations of past developments. He cannot be offering a more accurate interpretation of anything at all; he can only offer a more productive alternative based on (abstractly) restructured power-relations. In the case of sexuality, the present view of sex as repressed since the Victorian period is a construal which is a product of one set of power-relations. Foucault relates an alternative history which reveals the roles played by those power-relations, showing how sex was *not* repressed but rather shaped and developed in complex ways. He does so by highlighting just the things those operant power-relations sought to hide. But he is not claiming that history is wrong, that it is distorted by power-relations, for that would entail that someone might get it right because there was a series of events which occurred independently of interpretation-determining power-relations. There is no history independent of power-relations, because power-relations determine what is and is not history, as they determine what are and are not the events inventoried by history. The Foucauldian project embodies what is at the heart of postmodern critiques: that interpretation does go all the way down, that there is no separate bedrock, no neutral realm of facts or events beyond perception and values, which inquiry of any sort can get more or less right and which inquiry could conceivably get perfectly right.

This view looks frightening to many, for it seems to be a denial of all possibility of correctness, and so of justifiably judging something better than something else. But the resistance is somewhat difficult to explain. It has been a long time since truth was thought objective and absolute, at least by most theorists. This is most evident in the social sciences and some parts of the humanities, such as literary criticism and intellectual history. Even in the case of general history, the very existence of historiography shows that whereas at one time history's task was thought to be determining exactly what happened in the past, in the sense of capturing the precise sequence of objective events that made up a revolution or led to a war, we now understand too well the role of interpretation both in the identification of events and in description of those events. We understand that, say, the history of World War II looks very different to historians of the several combatant nations. There is, nonetheless, a tendency to make a distinction between the theoretical and abstract on the one hand, and the practical on the other, and to see the former but not the latter as open to varying interpretations. We really have not moved very far from the Cartesian perspective, because instead of abandoning or even seriously qualifying the Cartesian conceptions of truth and knowledge, we tend to purchase flexibility at the cost of impugning our own competence. That is, we blame our conceptual limits and methods of inquiry for whatever fallibility we have to accept. In other words, we keep Descartes's conceptions of truth and knowledge, but reconstrue truth as less readily discernible and knowledge as therefore less certain because possibly incomplete. In this way we try to allow for the undeniable plurality of viable interpretations of phenomena that interest us, while rather desperately reassuring ourselves that knowledge and truth are not so much unattainable as merely elusive.

What Foucault wants is for us to totally give up the Cartesian perspective, but not to give it up as merely wrong. That implies that there is a right perspective which we should pursue. He wants us to see the Cartesian perspective, which is itself the seeking of the correct perspective, as a product of a particular history and as unproductive and even counterproductive. To that end he provides us with alternative histories which differ radically from accepted ones. The aim of providing these alternative histories is only in part to win acceptance of particular reconstruals of the targeted practices or institutions or concepts. *The History of Sexuality* is only in part intended to defeat the view of sex as repressed and replace that view with one of obsessive interest in sex. The larger part of Foucault's aim is to show how different histories result in different practices, institutions, and concepts. His work on the prison in *Discipline and Punish* is, at one level, an effort to achieve reconstrual of the nature of penal institutions by revealing the relations of power which produce and are produced by our penal institutions. At another level it is an attempt to reveal how human beings come to be subjects of a certain sort and actually to conceive of themselves as such, how we have and do become self-monitoring subjects within certain regimes of power-relations. Foucault's work, then, is not only destructive with respect to some accepted notions, and productive with respect to new ones, it is descriptive with respect to how we shape ourselves as members of intellectual, social, political, and other institutions, and of how those institutions are developed and serve nonevident ends.

To understand the essential points in all this, one must appreciate the force of our case in point, *The History of Sexuality*, by understanding that our present sexuality is a particular construct, a specific conception, and one which could have been different. What Foucault does in *The History of Sexuality* is give a detailed account of how we came to have our present sexuality and just what that sexuality entails, how we came to conceive of ourselves as possessed of a certain sexuality, how we came to be the sexed and gendered entities we now are. But as I warned earlier, this is *not* to say that this sexuality is a construal of something given and independent, something—biological sex—which is as it is regardless of how we interpret it. The contention is that how we construe sexuality, *including* the very idea of what is supposedly more basic, namely biological sex, is determined by imposed norms and practices. And once it is understood that there are different possibilities with respect to conceptions of sexuality, Foucault's deeper message can be understood: that there are alternatives to all of our most basic construals. If something so supposedly basic as sexuality admits of alternative construal, we must at least consider that *everything* does. And this is the key to Foucault's importance for our purposes: by providing his radical alternative account of sexuality, and showing us that our sexuality is one among various possibilities and not just the one right or supposedly natural sexuality, what Foucault does is show us how an instance of knowledge is a product of history. Foucault's work thus denies Descartes's (and Plato's and Kant's) fundamental assumption that inquiry's aim is to discern and articulate that one correct construal of whatever is the object of our inquiry.

One of the major things we learn as Foucault makes out his case is that not only does philosophy not unearth truths, there is neither need nor room for philosophical theory in the way that Descartes offered a theory about how human error is a product of perfect will overriding limited intellect, or how to perceive is to entertain ideas and then make judgments about their representative nature, or how being human is a matter of being a substantial mind somehow attached to an extended body. For Descartes to philosophize was to theorize; for Foucault what needs doing is tracing and articulating the genealogy of whatever we find problematic.

The implication of this denial of depth is that nothing, whether sexuality or the behavior of subatomic particles, is in itself a subject of discourse. Nothing is a *natural* focus for study. This is because nothing is a particular something in itself. Unlike the view Descartes inherited, the world is not carved up into "natural kinds," into groupings of particulars that just are what they are by nature and must be apprehended as what they are. Objects of attention or inquiry are generated by our coming to objectify them in certain ways. For example, in the case of sexuality, we ourselves become objects of a certain sort, namely, entities possessed of a certain sexuality. And given that sexuality, all things, from articles of clothing to specifically delineated parts of our bodies to persons themselves, become objects of sexual interest and significance. Other examples are how we make our past an object of attention when we do what we then call "history," and how we make some of our own activities objects of attention which we take as comprising what we then call "political behavior." And how do we manage all of this? How do we make something a particular sort of object of attention? *By talking about it.* And when the talk becomes complex enough, we call it a "study" or a "discipline" and designate it— rather ironically—with a suffix, '-ology', which derives from the Greek 'logos', one of the various senses of which was "words said" or "discourse." (Guthrie, 1962:420–04) In this way we institutionalize and legitimize our talk about something and make that something an object of study. The results are "biology," "psychology," and so on.

The point of the foregoing paragraph is crucial for understanding Foucault. It is *discourse* that manufactures an object of inquiry and which then generates knowledge and truth about it. Discourse, and practice, make our world. Therefore, there is no occasion for deep theory that supposedly gets at underlying realities which explain the world or parts of it. All there is, all there can be, is careful tracing and mapping of how a discourse and its attendant practices develop. When we engage in Foucauldian genealogy, and understand how this or that came to be thought of and talked about and dealt with as it is, we learn all there is to learn about it. There is no deeper reality to be explored by special application of pure reason or arcane philosophical techniques. (It is worth mentioning, though, that Foucault's earlier work, prior to the late 1960s, which he called "archaeology," was concerned with unearthing something deep, with a sort of theorizing reminiscent of Cartesian methods and objectives. See Dreyfus and Rabinow, 1983.)

By now the reader will almost certainly be worrying that Foucault makes all values and even events and situations hopelessly relative. What must be understood at the outset is that if one feels Foucault merely relativizes everything, it is likely because the very standards Foucault is challenging are being applied to his claims. This is an elusive point, and if not stated carefully can be sophistical or as question-begging as what it is a response to, so let me make it in a different way. Descartes believed that with respect to any phenomenon, what we must do is analyze it to discern underlying truths and operant principles; Foucault is saying that whatever we might find in such a study we put there ourselves. This is not simply to relativize truth and knowledge, because the notions of relative truth and knowledge really only make sense if one accepts the meaningfulness of absolute truth and knowledge. Otherwise "relative" would have no contrast. Foucault is saying that what we take to be truth and knowledge are what they are because of history and power-relations, and there is no standard against which they can be only relative. Rorty makes the point very succinctly: "there is . . . no criterion that we have not created in the course of creating a practice, no standard of rationality that is not an appeal to such a criterion, no rigorous argumentation that is not obedience to our own conventions." (Rorty, 1982:xlii)

THE HISTORY OF SEXUALITY

O<small>UR</small> main concern here is not pursuing what Foucault has to say about the particular characteristics of socially determined institutions he finds of interest. What we want to do is appreciate the lesson his work teaches us, namely, that it will seem obvious and unquestionable to each person who employs a given construal of his world that he is a particular sort of subject. The point is that each person, each subject, is shaped by theory and practice, and it will seem natural to each practice- and theory-shaped subject that he *is* as he has come to take himself, and that the world *is* as he has come to take it. Further, we want to appreciate that it will seem natural to all subjects that each of their practice- and theory-shaped institutions is an inevitable development and a proper and delineated topic of investigation. All of this is a complex function of history and power-relations, and is illustrated by Foucault's demonstration of how a social construct is imposed as the very nature of human sexuality, and how that imposed sexuality is taken as an objective phenomenon requiring and supporting study and discussion. As he claimed in many of his interviews, Foucault has always been mainly concerned with power-relations—even though in his earlier work somewhat less clearly so. His studies of the clinic, madness, and the penal system can be seen as culminating in his genealogical treatment of sexuality. But the treatment of sexuality, while of great interest in itself, is essentially a means to an end: perhaps Foucault's clearest articulation of his position on power-relations.

The History of Sexuality begins with a chapter describing our time and culture as inheritors of the Victorian Age. The point at this early stage is to describe the received or accepted view which Foucault sets out to question and ultimately reject. In differentiating his own view from the traditional view, Foucault draws a crucial contrastive distinction between a "regime" of sexuality in which questions about sex and sexual behavior are raised in terms of what was *licit* and what *illicit*, in other words, according to or contrary to law, and a "regime" in which questions are raised in terms of what is *normal* and what *abnormal*. The latter is a greatly more complex situation, for it requires not only that there be established norms, but that they be internalized by those they range over. This is a major part of the contrastive distinction: in the case of law or even of externally imposed norms, individuals are coerced with respect to their actions. But in the case of thought, discourse and behavior governed by internalized norms, individuals are not coerced but self-regulated. The law-ruled regime is described by Foucault as a "deployment of alliances." The promulgation and enforcement of laws require alliances; they work only if groups and individuals enter into various arrangements and interdependencies—affiliations and associations that enable the coercion of others. In short, alliances facilitate the use of power as traditionally conceived, as domination. The norm-governed regime is described by Foucault in terms of the "deployment of sexuality," because what is deployed here are not various sorts of arrangements and compacts, but rather a particular *conception* which governs thought, discourse and behavior, not by coercion, but by creating sexuality as a certain sort of thing and people as certain sorts of agents.

The deployments of alliances and sexuality can be clarified by considering an example. For instance, in the alliances case, heterosexual intercourse and sodomy are legally sanctioned and legally prohibited acts, and what is common to them is that they are both acts falling within the purview of laws about sexual behavior. In the sexuality case, heterosexual intercourse and sodomy are instances of normal and abnormal sexual behavior, and that both are dealt with by the law is a secondary matter; primary is that they are both "expressions" of a single thing, *sexuality*, except that one is within the realm of "proper" sexual behavior while the other is not. In the regime of alliances, heterosexual intercourse falls under the purview of the law only in terms of attendant factors, such as age. Sodomy falls under the purview of law because it is deemed a crime. But in the regime of sexuality, heterosexual intercourse is conceived of as the paradigm of sexual activity, and sodomy is deemed abnormal, and a crime, in relation to that paradigm. But it is worth stressing that the deployment of alliances and sexuality contrast is not just one between law and norms. In the case of the deployment of alliances, where "sexual behavior" is what the law says it is, underage heterosexual intercourse and sodomy are both prohibited acts within the same law-determined reality. But in the case of the deployment of sexuality, where norms generated by a complex conception of sexuality determine the reality of sex, under-age heterosexual intercourse is a rather minor contravention of statutes, whereas sodomy is a *perversion* and hence in the broadest sense a medical concern. The two are different *sorts* of acts, they are in different categories, not categorized together simply by both being illicit. Foucault's contrast, then, is one between two *realities*; a reality in which diverse sexual activity is categorized and judged in relation to what is and is not *allowed*, and a reality in which sexual activity and sexuality itself are conceived in terms of what is and is not *natural*. There is need here to appreciate the implications of the difference in thinking of a sodomite as a *criminal* and thinking of a sodomite as a *pervert*.

Foucault proceeds by sketching how the seventeenth century saw a major shift in attitudes toward sex, basically one from candor and relative openness to one where sex was restricted to the familial context: "[a] single locus of sexuality was acknowledged . . . the parents' bedroom." (Foucault, 1980a:3) And as important as the circumscription of sexuality was the consequent creation, isolation, and restriction of deviancy to certain conditions and locales: "[t]he brothel and the mental hospital would be those places of tolerance: the prostitute, the client, and the pimp, together with the psychiatrist and his hysteric . . . seem to have surreptitiously transferred the pleasures that are unspoken into the order of things that are counted." (Foucault, 1980a:4) And this is where we begin to see that Foucault's concern goes beyond the alleged repression of sex postulated by the repressive hypothesis to the mechanics of whatever was going on under the guise of repression. There is a good indication of his later claims in the foregoing passage. Notice the reference to surreptitious transfer and the contrast between what is first merely unspoken and then is objectified and enumerated in the sense of being categorized and quantified. Categorization and quantification are pivotal to the process of inscribing sexuality in discourse, for these allow the merely unspoken to be classified in numerous orders of seriousness and distance from the norm. And these devices then enable their own application to the individuals engaging in the newly organized deviancy. The definition of "normal" procreational activity then requires corresponding definition of "abnormal" sexual behavior—which, given certain realities, must be tolerated to an extent. A direct consequence is that those who participate in abnormal sexual activity come to take themselves as deviants of one or another sort: victims of psychological disorders or compulsions or mere criminals. The development of discourse about sexuality, therefore, has enormous implications not only with respect to how sexual acts are conceived, but also how sexual agents are conceived. It is no surprise, then, that only a few pages later we are told that the general objective "is to define the regime of power-knowledge-pleasure that sustains the discourse on human sexuality," for there clearly is an extensive "regime" in place. (Foucault, 1980a:11) The objective must be to trace and articulate the devices by which objectification and enumeration are achieved, so that we may understand not only how and why sex is controlled, but also how it is construed as the sort of thing in need of control.

To this end Foucault raises three quite different questions. First is the historical question of whether there has been sexual repression. His answer will be, of course, that what has been deemed and presented as repression was actually an eruption of concern about and interest in sex. But this first question is quickly followed by two others: "Do the workings of power . . . really belong primarily to the category of repression? Did the critical discourse that addresses itself to repression . . . act as a roadblock to a power mechanism . . . unchallenged up to that point, or is it . . . part of the same historical network as the thing it denounces[?]" (Foucault, 1980a:10)

There are important indications here of what follows in *The History of Sexuality*. The second question sets the stage for reconception of power as not only repression or domination but something vastly more diffuse which permeates every aspect of our social being. The third question prompts us to consider that rather than discourse about power—in this case repression—having as its point the obstruction or mitigation of the use of power, it may actually function as an enabling condition for the use of power. The case in point is how the discourse on sex, through which sex was supposedly repressed, actually facilitated interest in sex by turning sex into an object of study and possible theorizing. This is why Foucault is setting out "to account for the fact that [sex] is spoken about, to discover who does the speaking. . . ." We are told that "[w]hat is at issue . . . is . . . the way in which sex is 'put into discourse.'" (Foucault, 1980a:11) But what merits repetition is that Foucault's is not a search for truth; he is not concerned "to formulate the truth about sex," nor is he concerned to expose the "falsehoods designed to conceal that truth." He seeks to understand what he calls the "will to knowledge" which shapes and supports what are taken as truths and falsehoods. (Foucault, 1980a:12)

The phrase, "the will to know," as noted in Part I, is the French title of *The History of Sexuality: Volume One*, but it, and its variant, "the will to knowledge," are dangerously misleading phrases. It may appear initially that the will to knowledge is, after all, a basically Cartesian conception: the will to learn the truth. But if the phrase is taken in this sense, the point of Foucault's work will be seriously missed. Foucault is precisely not speaking of knowledge as learning the truth. The whole point is to understand the structure of discourse that makes something count as knowledge and makes something count as truth. The will to knowledge is not a drive to discover the truth; the will to knowledge is a drive to establish a discourse. What Foucault wants to understand, then, is how we developed our discourse on sexuality and so made certain notions and ideas knowledge about sexuality: how we manufactured the truth of sex and sexuality, which we then reappropriate as knowledge about sex and sexuality. And here again one must guard against facile interpretation. Foucault is a very radical thinker, and much of what he says is radical enough that his readers tend to take it as much less so, inclining to think him only provocative or, as in the case of sexuality, detaching constructed sexuality from biological sex. And to further complicate matters, much of what he says is ironic. And irony is dangerous because it is often missed. Foucault saw it as fitting to use a phrase like "the will to knowledge" to designate not a striving for knowledge but the need to *create* knowledge. Appreciation of this irony will facilitate assimilation of what follows about *The History of Sexuality*.

The two short chapters titled "The Incitement to Discourse" and "The Perverse Implantation" provide us with the basic thesis of the repressive hypothesis and the gist of Foucault's conception of it. The essential point is that Foucault is not denying that there was, from roughly the latter half of the seventeenth century onward, a marked *policing* of sexual activity of all sorts. He does not deny that there was, for example, censorship. Foucault's point is that the policing was not in reality *repressive*; instead it masked "a veritable discursive explosion." (Foucault, 1980a:17) The social, political, and religious policing of sex was belied as real repression by the fact that at the level of "discourses and their domains, the opposite phenomenon occurred. There was a steady proliferation of discourses concerned with sex. . . . But more important was the multiplication of discourses concerning sex in the field of exercise of power itself: an institutional incitement to speak about it, and to do so more and more. . . ." (Foucault, 1980a:18)

Every restriction imposed carried with it more talk about its object. And each also carried with it certain sanctioned or at least tolerated displacements. Foucault uses confession as an example to stress that not only was admission of violations against sexual codes required, but detailed examination of those violations and their motivation was also demanded and became integral to alleged understanding of one's sexual being. That examination then served the purpose of not only furthering the discourse on sexuality, but of engaging the sexual agent in the increasing circumscription and scrutiny of sexuality. Through techniques such as confession the agents whose sexual activity was coming under ever greater control were made participants in the imposition of that control, and at the same time enabled to better bear the imposition of that control. Confession serves as a paradigm of the mechanisms used to control sexuality and to make the control bearable:

> This is the essential thing: that Western man has been drawn for three centuries to the task of telling everything concerning his sex; that since the classical age there has been a constant optimization and an increasing valorization of the discourse on sex; and that this carefully analytical discourse was meant to yield multiple effects of displacement, intensification, reorientation, and modification of desire itself. (Foucault, 1980a:23)

What Foucault describes is sexuality coming more and more under political control through the employment of technical vocabularies which defined and circumscribed sexuality in various ways, and the use of techniques which not only objectified sexuality but involved those to be controlled in the process of control.

The consequence of the elaboration of discourse on sexuality was that it became "not something one simply judged; it was a thing one administered." (Foucault, 1980a:24) Not only did the discursive treatment of sexuality circumscribe and control sexual attitudes and behavior, it made those attitudes and that behavior proper objects of administration by moral, religious, and secular institutions. Additionally it made sexuality a proper object of scientific study, and thereby rendered it vulnerable to the results of theoretical speculation. This latter meant that sexuality could be changed by theoretical developments, much as theory has numerous times changed the nature of "proper" childrearing.

In the second chapter of Part Two of *The History of Sexuality* Foucault is primarily concerned to demonstrate how the policing of sexuality, and its enshrinement in complex and often highly technical vocabularies, led to the phenomenon of the equally circumscribed and studied perversion. And we might here note a matter of terminology. For want of a better term, I spoke of the "policing" of sexuality to convey the idea of control which is not necessarily repressive. As we shall consider more carefully later, the proper Foucauldian term is the *governing* or *government* of sexuality. Unfortunately, this term has come to be very narrowly used in our time, so more material must be discussed before we employ it as Foucault does. To return to the point, Foucault goes to some lengths to show how transgressions and violations, previously only deplored, came to be classified and investigated and thereby became objects of even more intense study than "normal" sex. The overall thrust of Part Two, then, is the characterization of contemporary sexuality as a product not of natural attributes and behavior but of highly structured attitudes embodied and promulgated in technicalized discourse.

Part Three of *The History of Sexuality*, "Scientia Sexualis," is concerned with how sexuality became the subject matter of scientific inquiry and discourse. The central point here is that sexuality became "not only a matter of sensation and pleasure, of law and taboo, but also of truth and falsehood, [that] the truth of sex became something fundamental, useful, or dangerous, precious or formidable: in short, that sex was constituted as a problem of truth." (Foucault, 1980a:56) The title of the chapter highlights that our culture largely lacks an *ars erotica*, an artful treatment of sexuality. Instead our culture casts sexuality as the subject matter of scientific study, discussion, and control. The result is that sexuality becomes not an object for enhancement but a subject of inquiry. In our culture sexuality is something about which there are deep truths to be unearthed, and hence about which we can and must theorize. One consequence is that new power-relations arise which turn on greater or lesser knowledge, greater or lesser alleged mastery. It becomes possible, for instance, for some to become supposedly adept at understanding the sexual behavior of others and so at explaining that behavior in theoretical terms which the agents in question may not even recognize but are intimidated into accepting as descriptive of their own lives. The most important consequence of this is that a distinction is then drawn between the normal and the abnormal, and suddenly everyone is vulnerable to classification in terms of conformity or deviance, and so vulnerable to self-classification. Much of the point of *Discipline and Punish* is to show how the imprisoned come to conceive of themselves as persons of a particular sort and so as rightly subject to certain measures of control. *The History of Sexuality* shows how an imposed view of sexuality forces individuals to construe themselves as persons whose sexual inclinations are "proper" or "improper," normal or abnormal, and therefore how some of those individuals come to conceive of themselves as rightly subject to control against deviancy. And as we might expect, others conceive of themselves as empowered to exercise that control.

Things might not have been too bad if sexuality had in fact become only an object of scientific study. But as Foucault is at pains to establish early in Part Three, in the nineteenth century sex became not only an object of a biological study of reproduction, which adhered to established scientific principles and practices, but also a "medicine of sex." And the latter incorporated and thereby legitimated "age-old delusions" which were supposedly supported by a "distant and quite fictitious guarantee" extended by the biological study. (Foucault, 1980a:55) The constitution of sexuality as an issue of truth, then, had two distinct aspects, one which at least conformed to established scientific norms and one which amounted to little more than a grab-bag of biases and myths organized into a would-be discipline. Nor was the line too sharp. A quick look at the literature of the time suffices to show how even the most meticulous biologists and physiologists succumbed to the offering of editorial comments on sexuality and gender traits. Feminists, of course, are well aware of how science was and is used and bent to maintain and enhance sexual stereotypes. One important related development of this interweaving of science and institutionalized folklore, and hence the dubious employment of science, was that Sigmund Freud's (1856–1939) otherwise enlightening work was assimilated into the medico-psychiatric establishment, tailored to fit established expectations, and so controlled and prevented from prompting deeper examination of how sexuality worked. This development illustrates how power masks itself and how challenges to it are as often incorporated as resisted. Freud's work posed a serious challenge to the supposed repression of sexuality, and hence the deployment of sexuality, so Freudian theory had to be somehow assimilated into the dominant discourse, since it could neither be ignored nor conclusively refuted. The way in which Freud threatened the deployment of sexuality is somewhat indirect. Recall that in the distinction between the deployment of alliances and deployment of sexuality, a difference is marked between regimes based on law and on (internalized) norms. But Freud's work "rediscovered the law of alliance, the involved workings of marriage and kinship." (Foucault, 1980a:113) The trouble was that therefore it rediscovered the "guarantee that one would find the parents-children relationship at the root of everyone's sexuality. . . ." And this "made it possible . . . to keep the deployment of sexuality coupled to the system of alliance." (Foucault, 1980a:113) This meant that sexuality was "constituted only through the law," (Foucault, 1980a:113) and the deployment of sexuality would look a sham. In other words, the deployment of sexuality would appear to be what it actually was: the imposition of a discourse which unnecessarily recast sexuality in terms of norms and so on. The potentially most effective challenge to the deployment of sexuality, then, was dealt with not by rejection but precisely by assimilating Freud's work into the mechanics of that deployment through integration of his theories into accepted ones.

To return to our more general discussion of Part Three of *The History of Sexuality*, we have to note that the developments Foucault describes brought together two previously separate generative poles: a concern with the human species, and an interest in the human body. (Dreyfus and Rabinow, 1983:134–35) These were both enabling conditions and productive elements. As our human nature itself ceased to be problematic only as to whether it possessed a divinely imposed or an evolved nature, and became instead an object of diverse scientific study and speculation, not only were theories and explanatory concepts produced about human nature, but these theories and explanations were used as instruments of control of the body. This control began to be most evidently exercised in various specific areas where theory was applied to the management of people, such as in the prison. Foucault's *Discipline and Punish* is a detailed elaboration of this resulting practice.

We might briefly sum up the point in this way: as human beings themselves came under scientific, as opposed to only juridical and political scrutiny, and as scientific theories were generated about human nature and inclinations, juridical and political objectives were served by the new theories. For one thing, earlier repressive measures which had been legitimated only by the power of a monarch were made to seem legitimate by the very nature of those subjected to power. In the penal system, for instance, prisoners came to consider themselves subject to certain tendencies and so the appropriate objects of certain constraints; with respect to sexuality, men and women came to consider themselves possessed of certain traits and so the appropriate objects of certain constraints. And when we understand the complicitous roles of subjects, we appreciate the major point in Foucault's view that the exercise of power is most effective and best tolerated when masked. The key idea here is that the exercise of power is masked when those who are constrained are made to believe that it is something about themselves which requires the imposed constraints. And the most effective way of achieving this cognitive end, of getting people to believe that it is their own nature which calls for regulation, is to promulgate a "scientific" conception of human beings as having a specific objective nature, in the present case an objective sexuality, and so as objectively requiring control. Those who do the controlling are then made to seem mere servants of nature and necessity. As to what the more or less specific elements of constraint were, Foucault focuses on a number of things. As noted earlier, he makes much of the institution of confession. In the institution of the confession individuals are required to objectify and discuss their own inclinations, pleasures, fears and goals in ways that make these the proper subjects of theoretical analysis and assessment. Confession "is a ritual of discourse in which the speaking subject is also the subject of the statement; it is also a ritual that unfolds within a power relationship, for one does not confess without the presence (or virtual presence) of a partner who is not simply the interlocutor but the authority who requires the confession." (Foucault, 1980a:61) The process by which the individual comes to construe himself as a certain sort of sexed person is epitomized by the confession: "[t]he truthful confession was inscribed at the heart of the procedures of individualization by power." (Foucault, 1980a: 58–59)

The foregoing serves to remind us of our own special objective: the consideration of Foucault primarily as a counterpoint to Descartes. What is of special interest to us here is how very far we have come from a Cartesian conception that there is a truth to be discerned and articulated about the person, about what he is, and about what he knows and believes. Everything in *The History of Sexuality* reiterates the conception of the person as a construct, and of what he knows and believes as products, with no truth to be discerned or articulated. Instead there is a need to understand the mechanics of how a person comes to act as he does and to think of himself as he does.

Foucault provides a number of characterizations of procedures or devices by which individuals are molded into sexual beings of a particular sort. These are the "clinical codification of the inducement to speak," the "postulate of a general and diffuse causality," the "principle of a latency intrinsic to sexuality," a "method of interpretation," and the "medicalization of the effects of confession." (Foucault, 1980a:65–67) These sound rather more awesome than they are, and in any case are not of primary concern to us. However, this much can be said here about these devices: the clinical codification of the inducement to speak is basically an integration of confession and examination. Everything from tedious but non-threatening medical questionnaires through pointed interrogation to free association contributes to eroding the difference between a more or less factual record of an individual's treatment and his own perceptions and perspectives. He is made to see his most intimate thoughts as relevant to his record as a patient or even as a citizen. Much of the force behind this emphasis on revelation comes from the second device, the postulation of a diffuse causality, because it is the fostered view that sex can be the cause of almost anything which prompts complaints, and that only painstaking analysis can sort out causal influences. For instance even blindness and great pain can be only hysteria, and hysteria supposedly is caused most often by sexual disorders. A notorious and deplorably common case in point is "diagnosis" of women's complaints as due to, for example, menopause. And this understanding of sex as potential cause in almost any case of distress means that there is no limit to the degree of intimacy of questions which—in the most pertinent example—a health practitioner might ask, on the shared assumption that only total candor can enable effective diagnosis. The patient then actually wants to "tell all," because he sees it as necessary to understanding his malady and progressing toward a cure. The third device, the principle of a special latency intrinsic to sexuality, adds force: it makes it possible for practitioners and agents themselves to pursue the most elusive and difficult notions and desires on the assumption that the causes of sexual behavior are necessarily deeply buried. The fourth device, the method of interpretation, has to do with how what confession produces is treated and dealt with. The results of confession are not simply used in particular cases; they are interpreted as fitting pre-existent theory-dictated patterns. In this way, these products are both new material important to dealing with particular cases and corroboration of the operant theory. These products are not deciphered but rather enciphered in light of the operant theory. While the appearance is that of careful discernment of something already exhibiting a particular structure, what actually occurs is that what confession produces is precisely structured by the operant theory. This is how these results are then perceived as corroboration. Finally, the fifth device, the medicalization of the effects of confession, is the reconception of confession as therapeutic. Perhaps the most singularly important effect of this is that the products of confession come to be assessed not just in terms of perceived right and wrong, but in terms of the normal and the abnormal.

The upshot of all this is that,

> breaking with the traditions of an *ars erotica*, our society has equipped itself with a *scientia sexualis*. To be more precise, it has pursued the tasks of producing true discourses concerning sex. . . . The society that emerged in the nineteenth century . . . did not confront sex with a fundamental refusal of recognition. On the contrary, it put into operation an entire machinery for producing true discourses concerning it. (Foucault, 1980a:67–69)

It goes without saying that the last sentence would have made sense to Descartes only as referring to a program of deliberate deception, and so as the use of power conceived as domination. Descartes would have unhesitatingly endorsed the view that Foucault is most anxious to defeat, namely, the idea that "truth is intrinsically opposed to power and therefore inevitably plays a liberating role." (Dreyfus and Rabinow, 1983:127) For Descartes truth was the basic instrument of liberation, first from error, skeptical doubts and confusion, and by extension from what he would have seen as self-serving deception. The very idea that truth might itself be a *product* of power, that it might be no more—but no less—than what power makes it, would not have appeared to Descartes as just wrong or even inconceivable, but as actually pernicious. It would have been an idea worthy of the most diabolical efforts of the evil genius: the notion that truth not only was somehow manufactured by power, but could be of secondary importance to power. In contrast, for Foucault, what is pernicious is that we conceive of truth as liberating, as offering an alternative to lives and thought shaped by interactive relations, as if by gaining truth we could somehow be absolute beings of some kind, totally unrelated to others and the practices that in fact define us as individuals. What Foucault saw as pernicious was that this belief provoked endless and utterly fruitless struggle and the dissatisfaction that must inevitably accompany futility.

Part Four, titled "The Deployment of Sexuality," is where we find Foucault's most focused discussion of power-relations. This is the most important part of *The History of Sexuality*, in that it describes the deployment of sexuality, the manufacture or generation of our norm-based conception of sexuality against the earlier deployment of alliances or the law-based conception of sexual behavior. The four chapters that comprise this part are at once descriptive and expository. That is, Foucault offers a narrative description of how sexuality developed into what it is today, but he also makes basic claims about the nature of power-relations. As will be clear from what has been said so far, a good deal of what is claimed about power-relations is negative. This is partly because of the elusiveness and somewhat incomplete nature of Foucault's conception of power-relations, and partly because of his need to contrast his conception of power with the governing traditional conception of power as domination. Given our limited aims, we will here give the closest attention to what is said in Chapter Two of Part Four of *The History of Sexuality*, where perhaps the most explicit claims about power-relations are to be found.

Chapter One, "Objective," is descriptive not only of what Foucault intends to establish in this first volume of *The History of Sexuality*, but of the point of all six projected volumes. However, it is crucial that Foucault never intended to offer a theory of power; he sought to work out what he called an "analytics" of power-relations, something we might best think of as a dynamic description or conceptual map of power-relations. (Foucault, 1980a:82) "Foucault's account of power is not intended as a theory. [I]t is not meant as a context-free, ahistorical, objective description." (Dreyfus and Rabinow, 1983:184) As indicated earlier, it is to misconceive Foucault's project to take it as offering a competing theoretical framework. Such a framework might challenge established views, but it would not undermine them in the way that Foucault's postmodern contentions undermine traditional philosophy by reconceiving the objectivity traditional philosophy and science so tenaciously claim.

To better contrast his own conception of power-relations with it, Foucault dubs the traditional or domination view of power the "juridico-discursive" conception. (Foucault, 1980a:82) The force of this descriptive name is that the traditional conception is of power as coercive, prohibitive, and generally preventative and preclusive. Foucault's own notion of power-relations is one of an enabling set of relations, and the constraints it imposes are not always prohibitory but are sometimes permissive and promotive. That is, Foucauldian power constrains behavior not only by forbidding certain action but also by making some action inescapable or apparently appealing. To clarify this, let us briefly review the characteristics Foucault assigns to juridico-discursive power and which he contrasts with his own conception. First is the negativity of traditional power, exemplified in the fact that with respect to "sex and pleasure . . . power can 'do' nothing but say no to them." (Foucault, 1980a:83) This "cycle of prohibition" is the fact that traditional power over sexuality is exhausted by refusal and taboos. Second is the "insistence of the rule," or power conceived as essentially regulative, as classificatory with respect to the created categories of the licit and illicit, what is allowed and what is forbidden. Third is the "logic of censorship," which is basically a matter not only of rejection but also of denial. "The logic of power exerted on sex is the paradoxical logic of a law that might be expressed as an injunction of nonexistence, nonmanifestation, and silence." (Foucault, 1980a:84) It is not enough to prohibit certain acts; they must be denied existence. The accepted discourse of sexuality must eschew reference to numerous sorts of acts and desires. At best it can tolerate them only when they are couched in medical or theoretical terms. The most effective sort of censorship with respect to some sexual acts is to ensure lack of awareness of their existence or possibility. Fourth is the "uniformity of the apparatus," which is the consistency of denial, taboo and prohibition across classes and other distinctions in society. No one is exempt from the preventative and constraining application of traditionally conceived power to the sexual. And in each of the cases reviewed, power operates always as juridical: "it is a power . . . centered on nothing more than the statement of the law and the operation of taboos." (Foucault, 1980a:85)

The thrust of Chapter One of Part Four of *The History of Sexuality* is the point that is so thoroughly developed in *Discipline and*

Punish, that the traditional conception of power is that of a coercive restraining force best exemplified by prohibitive law. The traditional conception is a "Thou shalt not" conception, and the compulsion behind the prohibition is, of course, ultimately brute force. On this conception, those subjected to power are coerced and, as important, may be liberated, may be freed from the imposition of power. Liberation may come from greater, opposing power, but what concerns Foucault and us most is the traditional idea that liberation follows the discernment of truth. Recall our simple example about a nation described as warlike in a report. If we think of that report as an imposition of power, with resulting coercive consequences, we can see that on the traditional conception of power what is called for is that someone learn the truth about the nation in question, that someone learn whether the nation really is or is not warlike. But Foucault's lesson is that there just is no state of affairs that is the objective aggressiveness or non-aggressiveness of the nation, because these characterizations and their grounds are products of interpretation and are molded by history and interest.

We come now to Chapter Two of Part Four, "Method," in which we find the most positive and extended description of Foucauldian power-relations in *The History of Sexuality*. Having established the necessary contrast by describing the juridico-discursive conception of power, Foucault is now able to describe more constructively his own conception. We are offered a definition of power, but remember that Foucault has told us that he "hardly ever" uses the word 'power', and that if he does "it is always a short cut to the expression . . . relationships of power." (Bernauer and Rasmussen, 1988:11) We are told that "power must be understood . . . as the multiplicity of force relations immanent in the sphere in which they operate and which constitute their own organization; as the process which . . . transforms, strengthens, or reverses them; as the support which these force relations find in one another; and . . . as the strategies in which they take effect. . . ." (Foucault, 1980a:92–93) This definition will seem baffling if one approaches it with the traditional conception of power in mind, because the definition does not capture a unidirectional force; it is intended to capture something like a dynamic environment. Note the use of the phrase 'force relations'. Foucauldian power is not applied might or strength; rather it is a tissue of interacting enabling conditions and constraints. We will consider this definition more carefully in the section on power; for now the important thing is to appreciate the complex, dynamic, and essentially reciprocal nature of Foucauldian power-relations.

It could be argued that the use of 'power', both by Foucault using English and by his translators, is unfortunate, but it is hard to see what term would have been preferable. In any case, the same conceptual difficulties arise in French, so we cannot blame lack of clarity on mistranslation. The fact is that Foucault's notion of power is elusive, and he likely would have developed it more fully and clearly had he lived longer. The best we can do is to emphasize this "environmental" interpretation, to think of power as a dynamic set of interrelations which constrain by promoting some thoughts and actions and inhibiting others. What is of greatest importance is to maintain the contrast with the traditional juridico-discursive or coercive-dominance conception. It is less important that Foucault's own conception be wholly worked out than that we appreciate the inadequacy of power conceived only as domination and as unidirectional.

Obviously Foucault's notion of power is demanding and central to his thought. For that reason, as just promised, I devote a separate section to it, and we can here proceed with our brief review of *The History of Sexuality*. Chapter Three, "Domain," centers on a list of four elements which Foucault identifies in the production of contemporary sexuality. These are, first, the "hysterization of women's bodies" or reconception of women as essentially and thoroughly sexual beings, as "saturated with sexuality" and hence prone to a multitude of related infirmities; second, the "pedagogization of children's sex" or reconception of children as "preliminary" sexual beings requiring the strictest control to avoid abnormality; third, the "socialization of procreative behavior" or circumscription of the heterosexual pair as the productive element of society; and fourth, the "psychiatrization of perverse pleasure" or the creation and development of categories of abnormality and of corrective techniques relative to the emergent conception of normal sexuality. (Foucault, 1980a:104–05) These strategic elements are what led to "the very production of sexuality." (Foucault, 1980a:105) This third chapter of Part Four has the gist of the socio-historical thesis of *The History of Sexuality*, the claim that the elements Foucault describes were produced by the discourses which developed from the late seventeenth century on. This is where we find the basic constructivist claims about how contemporary sexuality is a product of discourse and how the repression of sexuality never occurred but was only a device in the development of the discourse, of a new set of power-relations.

The fourth chapter of Part Four, "Periodization," is of lesser interest to us. In it Foucault describes the historical progression of the development of present sexuality, with some emphasis on the role of social class in that development. What merits mention here is that against his own Marxist ideological background, and the ideological climate of France and most of Europe at the time, Foucault argued contrary to mainstream Marxists that rather than "repression of . . . the classes to be exploited," the deployment of sexuality was "self-affirmation" of the bourgeoisie. (Foucault, 1980a:122) Instead of restricting sex to the productive business of procreation and stopping it being a counterproductive distraction, the "hegemonic" class institutionalized its special status and "provided itself with a body to be cared for, protected, [and] cultivated . . . with . . . a technology of sex." (Foucault, 1980a:122)

As is the case with the fourth chapter, most of Part Five of *The History of Sexuality* does not require recapitulation here, given our limited purposes. The following passage, though, deserves special attention:

> Power would no longer be dealing simply with legal subjects over whom the ultimate dominion was death, but with living beings, and the mastery it would be able to exercise over them would have to be applied at the level of life itself; it was the taking charge of life, more than the threat of death, that gave power its access even to the body. For millennia, man remained what he was for Aristotle: a living animal with the additional capacity for a political existence; modern man is an animal whose politics places his existence as a living being in question. (Foucault, 1980a:142–43)

Here again, as in the case of biological sex, Foucault is making a claim which will seem startling in that it seems to deny or ignore the given. He is claiming that contemporary science and technology have made the existence of human beings a political issue, but not only in the sense that technology has put us at risk of annihilation. He is more concerned with the "us" that are at risk. Foucault is again contending that our existence, both as subjects and as beings of a certain kind, is a product of discourse, practice and history. And again Foucault wants us to understand that it makes no sense to think and talk about our "brute" existence as human beings, for that is to postulate a reality accessible only from a God's-eye point of view, and hence one which it makes no sense to affirm or deny.

Instead we have to understand that, for instance, the newly-gained capability of wiping out human life with nuclear warfare has made our existence as human beings a political matter, and in the process we have become subjects of yet another discourse, one about human beings in danger of annihilation. And to that extent, we have been defined *as* subjects yet again and in a new way.

It bears mention that this review of *The History of Sexuality* is intended less as detailed exposition than as an outline to guide reading of that text. Recall that this book will be incomplete without thorough reading of both Descartes's *Meditations* and Foucault's *The History of Sexuality*. The quotations and exegetical remarks made here are not intended and cannot begin to substitute for careful reading of those works. But to continue our consideration of *The History of Sexuality*, it is now necessary to look rather more closely at the Foucauldian notion of power-relations and how it relates to our main concern: understanding the extreme alternative conceptions of knowledge and truth represented by Descartes and Foucault.

POWER

In sharp contrast to the detailed ge-
nealogical account of sexuality, the discussion of power is more
implicit than explicit in *The History of Sexuality*. The relatively few
passages in which power as such is specifically considered are brief
and sometimes cryptic, as is evident from those quoted above.
Nonetheless, it is not too much to say that power is the real topic
of *The History of Sexuality*. If the key philosophical idea in Descartes's
work is that of objective truth, and so of knowledge as possession
of truth, the key notion in Foucault's work is that of power, and
of knowledge as the product of power. We must now focus more
directly on that notion of power. But as is inevitable in dealing with
Foucault, a certain indirectness is necessary. We have to begin with
consideration of the sense in which sexuality, or any similar institution or phenomenon, is a *product*. A key passage, part of which
was quoted earlier, will serve as our point of departure:

> The object . . . is to define the regime of power-knowledge-pleasure
> that sustains the discourse on human sexuality. . . . The central
> issue . . . [is] to account for the fact that [sex] is spoken about, to
> discover who does the speaking, the positions and viewpoints from
> which they speak, the institutions which prompt people to speak about
> it and which store and distribute the things that are said. What is at
> issue . . . is the overall "discursive fact," the way in which sex is "put
> into discourse." (Foucault, 1980a:11)

Note how this passage highlights the nature of the Foucauldian
project in *The History of Sexuality* in particular, but also in general.

The phenomenon addressed by Foucault, sexuality, is a cultural product; it is, in short, the complex whole of what we have come to think and say and do regarding sex. What is examined is how sex is spoken (and thought) about, who and what we are as speakers and agents when we speak about and engage in sex, what our presuppositions and operating principles are when we speak about sex, and how we promulgate and enforce our views on sex. The conclusions which the Foucauldian project supports will always be about what people think and say and do, not about some inaccessible and therefore unthinkable underlying facts of human biology and a distinct attitudinal overlay. We are launched, then, on a project concerned with basic interpretation, one which repudiates the notion of brute reality, construing any idea of such a reality as itself a product of interpretation. This is difficult, because we tend to insist on asking what it is that is interpreted, imagining that there must be an objective matter for interpretation. But that is to misconceive the Foucauldian position and project; it is still to imagine that the world is a "raw" given which we interpret in diverse and even incompatible ways. What must be appreciated is that even if there were a reality accessible only from a God's-eye point of view—again, from *no* point of view—it would have *nothing to do* with what we think and say and believe, because such a brute reality is inconceivable to us. All we can do, then, is painstakingly trace how a given reality came to be as it is. (It may now be clearer why I said earlier that Descartes would have thought Foucault mad or a charlatan. But that may say more about Descartes's mode of philosophizing than about Foucault.)

In the next section we will consider more carefully the produced nature of sexuality, but it suffices to proceed with our consideration of power that one accept, at least tentatively, that sexuality is somehow a product, and that one be prepared to ask what it is a product *of*. The foregoing quoted passage tells us that the immediate answer is "discourse." However, that seems less than clear or sufficient. We need to know more about the "regime" which "sustains" the discourse. And that means finding out more about power. As we proceed, it is again worth recalling that our interest in *The History of Sexuality* is in the philosophical import of what Foucault has to say. It is too easy to get caught up in consideration of Foucault's specific claims about sexuality and to overlook the conceptual and methodological implications. Our immediate concern is with what Foucault implies about knowledge; it is only secondarily with what Foucault says about sexuality. Foucault is here being juxtaposed to Descartes with the primary intent of clarifying the contrast between an objectivist and a constructivist view of knowledge, truth and philosophical inquiry. Throughout the reading of Foucault one must approach his claims first as examples of a way of thinking and writing, and only secondarily as substantive contentions.

There are a number of negative points we can make about Foucauldian power by way of trying to get clear on what is admittedly an elusive notion—a notion which some argue is ultimately incoherent. (Taylor, 1986) First, as already stressed, Foucauldian power is not to be identified with domination, as power almost invariably is. "Power comes from below; that is, there is no binary and all-encompassing opposition between rulers and ruled at the root of power-relations, and serving as a general matrix." (Foucault, 1980a:94) This first point is crucial. It must be understood that for Foucault power is not a one-way relation between those with power and those subject to power. We are explicitly told that power is not something which an individual or a group simply has and exerts on another. Power "is not something that is acquired, seized, or shared, something that one holds on to or allows to slip away; power is exercised from innumerable points, in the interplay of non-egalitarian and mobile relations." (Foucault, 1980a:94) Things are vastly more complex than one or a few exerting domination over others. As I suggest above, power is more like an environment in which practices are enabled and inhibited: practices which, by being conducted, contribute to power. Here we need to look again at the definitional passage on power, part of which was quoted earlier. This is the fullest definitional statement on power in *The History of Sexuality*, and so is of obvious importance. Foucault tells us that

> power must be understood in the first instance as the multiplicity of force relations immanent in the sphere in which they operate and which constitute their own organization; as the process which, through ceaseless struggles and confrontations, transforms, strengthens, or reverses [force relations]; as the support which these force relations find in one another, thus forming a chain or a system, or on the contrary, the disjunctions and contradictions which isolate them from one another; and lastly, as the strategies in which they take effect, whose general design or institutional crystallization is embodied in the state apparatus, in the formulation of the law, in the various social hegemonies. (Foucault, 1980a:92–93)

Power is not a something. Not only is it not unidirectional, it is not anything at all in the sense of something that can be *possessed*.

Foucault persistently stresses the dynamic nature of the notion, and in a passage that nicely summarizes the foregoing, he tells us that "power is not an institution, and not a structure; neither is it a certain strength we are endowed with; it is the name that one attributes to a complex strategical situation in a particular society." (Foucault, 1980a:93) We begin to see, then, the force of talking about a "regime." What we are dealing with is a dynamic structure, not a directed force or a static set of regulations or conventions or a persisting institution. The structure in question is decidedly dynamic. Power is never simply actual or otherwise; it is a shifting, changing set of relations. We can freeze these relations in abstraction, and then describe particular aspects of the relations as individuals or groups having power over others. But when we do so, we extract an ideational construct from real and active developments. It is as if we take a photograph of a single moment or event in an ongoing activity. In saying that a certain individual or group "has" power over others we abstract from a highly complex situation in which the person or group said to have power is equally, though perhaps in a very different and subtle manner, constrained by those over whom that person or group is said to have power.

Power is not only not domination and not something possessed; it is not exercised as a distinct activity. This is because it is not something *separate* from other relations: "[r]elations of power are not in a position of exteriority with respect to other types of relationships. . . ." (Foucault, 1980a:94) But more perplexing for the beginner or the traditional philosopher is that for Foucault power is not always and necessarily some*one's* power in the sense in which we understand power as always requiring an agent, that is, someone who has or exercises power in his own right or as the instrument of a group or class. Not only is power not separable from other relationships, it is not always identifiable with a particular individual's intentions or activity. Foucault tells us that "if it is true that Machiavelli was among the few . . . who conceived the power of the Prince in terms of force relationships, perhaps we need to go one step further, [and] do without the persona of the Prince, and decipher power mechanisms on the basis of a strategy that is immanent in force relationships." (Foucault, 1980a:97) This is a point which Foucault is intent on making in spite of the great resistance it prompts—to the extent that because of it some think Foucault's notion of power to be incoherent. (Taylor, 1986) Power is not anyone's; it is not something that one can gain, have, use and lose. What is important about this admittedly difficult idea is that power is not something circumscribed in such ways that it can be possessed. To act in any way is to exercise power, for it is to directly or indirectly constrain the behavior of others. Additionally, to be passive is not only to be subject to power. It is also to exercise power in the sense that one's passivity itself constrains the behavior of others. Consider, for instance, the whole point and the real effectiveness of passive resistance in the political sphere. Foucauldian power, then, is what enables the exercise of what we ordinarily call power, for it provides the context or matrix within which someone behaves in ways described as having domination over another, and within which someone is described as dominated.

Perhaps this much can be said here by way of clarification: human beings, as agents, are capable of behavior of nearly infinite variety. If a person were totally alone and, *per impossibile*, his behavior not determined by socially internalized beliefs, he would be free of Foucauldian power. But he would also not be a social being or agent. The moment we introduce even one other person, our exemplary free individual becomes a social agent and his behavior is constrained by the presence and actions of the other person. He is then in the realm of Foucauldian power: he participates in Foucauldian power because his behavior is constrained both by the actions of the other and by his own beliefs and expectations regarding the other. Of course his actions reciprocally constrain the behavior of the other, as do the beliefs and expectations the other has regarding him. "The term 'power' designates a relationship between partners." (Dreyfus and Rabinow, 1983:217) But to repeat, the relationship of "partnership" is not one of coercion or domination or force. If one person acts in such a way as to make another see himself, his options and possibilities, and his world, in certain ways, the first exercises power over the second without doing anything as crude as coercing the second. Our peers constantly exercise power over us because their expectations, their values, and their perceptions of and reactions to us are of specifiable sorts, but they do not coerce us. A good example is something I have made much of elsewhere, namely, how a person in his late fifties comes to be perceived and dealt with by others as someone whose age has begun to limit him in various ways. (Prado, 1986) The aging person may not yet be limited in the ways in question, but he may come to *accept* that he is, because of how he is perceived and dealt with. In this way, our culture imposes extremely unfortunate Foucauldian constraints on the elderly, due to the dubious conception of what it is to grow and be old. An aging person, in our present culture, is one whose self-perception, expectations, fears and hopes are shaped largely by external social influences. And the way this happens highlights the impersonal nature of Foucauldian power, because in spite of the fact that individual agents are involved, the power that shapes the elderly person's beliefs is not power wielded by *particular* individuals with a specific aim in mind.

The impersonal nature of Foucauldian power explains why there can be "no escaping from power . . . it is always already present, constituting that very thing which one attempts to counter it with." (Foucault, 1980a:82) One cannot escape power, one cannot be free, by getting away from any given person or any given institution. To be free one would have to be utterly solitary and to also somehow shed all the enculturation and conditioning that make one a social being. There is no Cartesian core self to be liberated, for liberation of that sort is annihilation of the person. The point about the inherent reciprocity of power-relations is perhaps clearest in that even when one is most blatantly and impotently subject to the exercise of power in the ordinary sense, as when forced to do something, one exercises Foucauldian power. This is because even as a victim one nonetheless constrains the behavior of the dominator, and because as a victim one is a player in the game of human interrelations, and as such one partly defines a power relation. Even the most abject victim constrains the behavior of his victimizer. This constraint may not be a curbing of the victimization; in fact it may actually increase that victimization. But the point that concerns Foucault is that by being a victim a person participates in a power relation. Just to the extent that the victim's response and suffering either temper the actions of the victimizer or goad the victimizer to greater excess, the victim constrains the action of the other and so participates in a power relation. This point may be elusive, or even repugnant, when we try to think of brutally victimized individuals as somehow engaged in a power relation, but it is crucial to appreciate it so as not to confuse Foucauldian power with domination. Foucault insists that "[w]here there is power, there is resistance, and yet . . . this resistance is never in a position of exteriority in relation to power." (Foucault, 1980a:94–95) Resistance is not something distinct from power, which can either occur or not occur where there is power. Even a wholly passive person offers resistance in the sense that he partly defines the power-relation and so inescapably constrains the behavior of the dominator, though not necessarily in a way beneficial to himself.

The ubiquity and inescapability of Foucauldian power clarifies the last negative point to be made here, which is that we do not find power only where we find evident or even covert domination, whether the domination be lawful or otherwise: "the new methods of power [are] not ensured by right but by technique, not by law but by normalization, not by punishment but by control." (Foucault, 1980a:89) Power is greatly more extensive than domination and comprises "methods that are employed on all levels and in forms that go beyond the state and its apparatus." (Foucault, 1980a:89) Power does not always come labeled, as in the case of the evident power of the state, or of a particular agency like the police, or of an employer. The bulk of power is to be found in much subtler forms: in influences and constraints which mask themselves as social consensus or tradition or expectations of "reasonable" behavior. Power is not necessarily legislated or ostensively assigned or created; it is not necessarily a product of either contract or might. Instead it is a diffuse enabling and inhibiting environment within which certain acts are then instances of domination and submission.

This enabling role of power is perhaps the most crucial to Foucault's work, and this is most clearly illustrated in *The History of Sexuality*. Foucault tells us that if "sexuality was constituted as an area of investigation, this was only because relations of power had established it as a possible object; and conversely, if power was able to take [sexuality] as a target, this was because techniques of knowledge and procedures of discourse were capable of investing it." (Foucault, 1980a:98) In other words, certain behavior and varied relationships constitute a set of power-relations which become a focus of attention and study. These power-relations facilitate the objectification of sexual behavior as a structured whole, as human sexuality. Sexuality then becomes something capable of being a subject of study; it is made into the subject matter of scientific inquiry, and so of control. Sexuality is objectified in discourse and made the object of a multifaceted "technology." The contentious surveys of sexual behavior by Alfred Kinsey (Kinsey, 1948–53), which were perhaps the first widely popularized studies of sexuality in North America, provide a good example of how what was previously intensely personal suddenly became the subject of widespread discussion, how something initially taken as disparate urges and inclinations and their consequences was objectified as a universal but problematic web of traits and behavior which pre-exist and define human sexuality. Conversely, it was only because men and women enter into relations of power among themselves as gendered individuals that there were activities and complex sets of power-relations which could be focused on as "human sexuality." The existence and consistency of certain relational activities provided a focus, and the objectification of those activities as of a given sort enabled them to become a subject of study and of specialized discourse.

It is just here that our interest is greatest. For Descartes, subjects of intellectual inquiry were natural kinds that simply existed as given types and which invited and sustained study. But for Foucault, every subject of study is a product, an artifact. Moreover, whereas for Descartes study was reasoned effort at discernment of the objective traits and features of the subject of study, and study aimed at accurate description of that wholly objective subject of study, for Foucault it is study itself which both constitutes the subject studied and bestows on it whatever objectivity it is thought to have. The subject of study does not pre-exist the study, but develops as a consequence of the discourse that sustains the study. This is the contrast I have alluded to several times: for Descartes intellectual inquiry is quite literally a search, hence it is a search for what is already there but which happens not to be evident. For Foucault intellectual inquiry is the manufacture of what Descartes sought to find. The role of power in the manufacture of subjects is highly complex; there is a reciprocity between power and knowledge, a wholeness that makes them aspects of the same thing rather than different things. This is why Foucault often speaks of "power-knowledge" and insists that "there is no exteriority" between "techniques of knowledge and strategies of power." (Foucault, 1980a:98) All behavior involves power-relations, all power-relations generate knowledge. In the next section we will look more closely at how power produces truth with respect to sexuality.

Keeping in mind that sexuality is only a case in point, exemplifying how anything we might describe as "an institution" comes to be as it is, we can close this section by looking once more at the definitional passage referred to above in order to fill out the account of Foucauldian power a bit more. Power is (1) a "multiplicity of force relations" which somehow (2) "constitute their own organization." But power is also (3) "the process which . . . transforms" these force relations. So power is both a self-sustaining dynamic structure and the intricate inherent mechanisms which alter the structure. And power is not only this set of interactive force relations, but also the procedures by which they are altered. We are further told (4) that power is also "the support which these force relations find in one another . . . [and/or] . . . the disjunctions and contradictions which isolate them from one another." And there is still more, for power is also (5) "the strategies in which [force relations] take effect." (Foucault, 1980a:92–93) These last two elements mean that the self-sustaining, internally developing multiplicity of force-relations incorporate and are actually constituted by elements some of which are mutually supportive and some mutually exclusive. The alterations of the multiplicity of force relations, of the dynamic structure these force relations comprise, will therefore be somewhere the results of constituents which reinforce one another, and elsewhere the results of constituents which diminish or obliterate other constituents.

Recall that we are not talking here about how something independent influences human interaction. The whole idea is that power is not a separate *something* in that sense. When we say, in genealogical detail, how human beings interact, we say all there is to how power enables and controls human interaction. As the above elements should make clear, Foucauldian power is not anything over and above how human interactions structure themselves. This is a hard lesson for Westerners, who tend always to reify abstractions, to think of them as things, albeit of a special sort. A parallel might be drawn with friendship; friendship is not anything over and above the special relations among certain people. This parallel would clarify Foucauldian power, except that friendship is vulnerable to the same reification. Whole books may be written about friendship with scarcely a mention of particular friendly relations between particular individuals. We ought not to think of friendship as a something somehow detachable from specific, multitudinous relationships, but we do. And while we ought not to think of Foucauldian power as distinct from what is captured by painstakingly detailed genealogies of specific force relations, too many people do. What can be said in the abstract has been said in the foregoing quoted passage; any more must be precisely what we are offered in *The History of Sexuality* and *Discipline and Punish*: detailed accounts of actual developments. Power structures human interaction only in the sense that all instances of human interaction are instances of Foucauldian power or structured force relations. Nothing external imposes itself on our actions; we just act in certain ways *vis-à-vis* one another. In a word, our interactions are not so much structured by anything as occur in structured ways.

As alluded to earlier, Foucault uses the archaic sense of the term "government" to describe the structuring role of power. (Allen, 1991) This is a sense which was considerably broader than the present largely political sense, a sense which meant management, regulation, and administration of anything calling for such. Unfortunately these latter terms have, in their modern uses, themselves come to operate more narrowly than in the past. The point Foucault wants to make is that power manages and regulates, but in a broader sense than that in which a government and its various agencies regulate every sort of civil activity.

> Basically power is . . . a question of government. This word must be allowed the very broad meaning which it had in the Sixteenth Century. 'Government' did not refer only to political structures or the management of states; rather it designated the way in which the conduct of individuals or states might be directed: the government of children, of souls, of communities, of families, of the sick. [Government] did not cover only the legitimately constituted forms of political or economic subjection, but also modes of action, more or less considered and calculated, which were designed to act upon the possibilities of action of other people. To govern, in this sense, is to structure the possible field of actions of others. (Dreyfus and Rabinow, 1983:221)

To govern is to structure possible actions. This notion of structuring behavior is the key one to understand in grasping Foucault's notion of power. In particular it is important that whereas power in the familiar sense of domination focuses on individuals by coercing or inhibiting persons, Foucauldian power, as an enabling and restricting environment, focuses on action: "the exercise of power is . . . a way in which certain actions modify others. . . . [W]hat defines a relationship of power is that it is a mode of action which does not act directly and immediately on others. Instead it acts upon their actions. . . ." (Dreyfus and Rabinow, 1983:219–20)

A great deal of the opposition to Foucault centers, first, on how power can be a "mode of action" that is not assignable to particular individuals with determinate intentions and abilities to enforce their will, and, second, on the question of the mechanics of this mode of action. The simplest thing we can say in response to worries about the lack of assignation of power is that it really does not matter, for any individual would do as the object of attribution, if he were in the right circumstances. It is context and circumstances that matter, not particular agents. As for the actual mechanics of power, the bulk of Foucault's work is precisely the illustration of those mechanics—how power works in the clinic, the asylum, the prison. As I have stressed before, the postmodern thrust of Foucault's work is that there is neither need nor room for theorizing of the traditional sort; that all we can do is trace and articulate genealogical accounts of the operant roles of power in given contexts. Foucault sees theoretical accounts as themselves the results of power. A theoretical account of the development of the prison, for instance, as part of some postulated inevitable historical process, would itself be a prime candidate for genealogical depiction and explanation. Remember that our main interest is in the contrast between Foucault and Descartes, and this is nowhere more evident than in the reason for Foucault's rejection of traditional theorizing, which is precisely because "power perpetually creates knowledge" and not the other way around. (Foucault, 1980b:51–2)

TRUTH AND SEXUALITY

> The important thing is that truth isn't outside power, or lacking in power: truth isn't the reward of free spirits . . . nor the privilege of those who have succeeded in liberating themselves. Truth . . . is produced only by virtue of multiple forms of constraint. Each society has its regime of truth . . . that is, the types of discourse which it accepts and makes function as true; the mechanisms and instances which enable one to distinguish true and false statements, the means by which each is sanctioned; the techniques and procedures accorded value in the acquisition of truth; the status of those who are charged with saying what counts as true. (Foucault, 1980b:131)

Most would acknowledge that etiquette is a social construct in the sense that the rules that govern the various practices that comprise most of social behavior are made by us, and are neither natural nor objective. Aside from a motivating basic courtesy and interest in smooth interaction, nothing underlies the structures of these practices. The specifications of the various etiquette practices do not call for study except of the purely descriptive sort. That is, a researcher might be concerned to study how a particular cultural group conducts introductions of strangers or how they eat in public, or just how these practices developed, but no one would think it appropriate to try to discern what the universally right way is to conduct an introduction or to hold a fork. It is understood that it is we who determine these things through our preferences and habitual actions; they are not determined by some objective nature. There is, then, nothing more to understand once we understand how the relevant procedures came about and are conducted. Matters of etiquette are spoken of as "purely conventional." What this means is that they are governed by fluid and flexible rules which derive from what people do and would like to do, and not anything deeper. These rules are occasionally compiled and even rationalized by those who take an interest in them, and these compilations acquire a certain normative force, witness the popularity and relative effectiveness of etiquette books and advisory newspaper columns. But there is no theorizing about the origins and nature of these rules beyond historical accounts of their adoption and promulgation.

In the case of sexuality there is an extensive cognitive dimension integral to the identification, collection and study of sex-related activities under the rubric of "human sexuality." Unlike in the case of etiquette, it came to be readily accepted that there are deep truths to be unearthed about sexuality. And together with this acceptance went the assumption that we have cognitive techniques for discerning those truths. Sexuality came to be not just a topic for detailed descriptive study, but the "natural" subject of various highly sophisticated investigative disciplines and technologies. Sexuality came to be a proper subject matter for specialized methods of investigation to discern its objective nature, and so of control and manipulation rather than only description and possible alteration. But for Foucault, sexuality is a social construct, and the primary concern of intellectual inquiry is not discerning the nature of sexuality but understanding how it came to be thought of as it is, and also as anything other than practice-constituted in its entirety.

Foucault's *The History of Sexuality* operates at two quite distinct levels: first, there is what is actually said and claimed about sexuality and the repressive hypothesis as the book's ostensive subjects; second, there is what is consistently and rather relentlessly implied about intellectual inquiry in general and philosophy in particular. What is said about sexuality has two aspects or dimensions. There is the contentious thesis which is the book's central one, that rather than being repressed sexuality has flourished as the topic of popular and learned discourses. There is also the apparently secondary but actually primary thesis that power-relations define and are manifest in how individuals are shaped and their behavior determined by how they see themselves and are seen within the confines of practice-determined roles and the expectations of their peers. In this particular book the roles and expectations are gender and sex-related, but the same message is found in *Discipline and Punish*, where the roles and expectations have to do with penal-system practices and control of those who are imprisoned. Any one of these points provides abundant material for thought and discussion, but what interests us is that in the process of making his claims about sexuality, Foucault effectively paints a picture of cognitive activity as productive rather than purely investigatory. Foucault thereby provides a richly suggestive counterpoint to Cartesian assumptions and methods by claiming that we create what we then take as given or determinate. And he goes on to show us how we bestow on the products of our creative practices the status of objectivity. As has been said a number of times, for Descartes, intellectual inquiry was investigation into a subject matter itself independent of our wondering and searching; for Foucault, intellectual inquiry is a productive and determining exercise which is as much responsible for the nature and existence of what it focuses on as it is for what is learned about its topics. Foucault's productive conception of intellectual inquiry is diametrically opposed to our theoretical, pedagogical, and investigatory traditions, and it is therefore as difficult to fully understand as it is important. It is a hard idea for most of us to take seriously, much less accept, that rather than discovering truth through investigation, we are instead "subjected to the production of truth through power. . . ." (Foucault, 1980b:93)

The creative or productive conception of inquiry is clearest when Foucault tells us that "sex was constituted as a problem of truth." (Foucault, 1980a:56) Sexuality is not a given with which we eventually must come to terms; it is not a determinate aspect of being human about which we can learn. Rather, sexuality is how we construe all that we do and say when we act as sexed creatures, *including* the idea of our being objectively sexed creatures. Had our history been different, sexuality might never have been an isolable area of special concern and investigation. It is possible that sexual activity might have been of fairly negligible interest or, more likely, been very differently construed. We can imagine, for instance, a culture which categorizes what we consider sexual behavior as various distinct sorts of activities, and is indifferent to whether sexual functions are performed privately or publicly, as our culture is indifferent to whether one eats in private or in public. Imagine further that this possible culture, which is indifferent to whether *sexual* activity is public or private, considers anything involving *cognitive* activity, such as learning, to be inherently private. It might be thought, for complex historical reasons, that activities through which an individual alters or enhances his beliefs are most properly private and must be conducted in strict isolation to minimize confusing or distorting external influences. Whereas we restrict sexual activity to the private realm and have massive public educational establishments, the imagined culture would have public sexual activity but restrict education to the privacy of the home or to limited-access facilities comparable to our public washrooms. Foucault himself describes eighteenth and nineteenth century schools and penal-system education where pupils were made to sit in enclosures open only at the front which physically isolated them from other pupils and directed their attention solely on the instructor. (Foucault, 1977) In our imagined culture, the isolation of learners would be much more strict and would preclude the role of the teacher. Very young children would be taught to read by their parents, and education would henceforth be solitary. What we now know as correspondence course education would be the norm, and the idea of a class or a public lecture would be thought lewd and offensive.

In the imagined culture, education would constitute an even more complex and compelling topic for discussion and study than it does in our culture, for its private nature would add complicating aspects which we can only guess at. But the point is that highly privatized education would be a subject matter taken as arising naturally from the "objective" natures of learning and of social interaction, and a perceived need to satisfy the requirement for purity in the learning process. Intellectual inquirers in the imagined culture would be concerned to better understand the ideally private nature of education in order to develop more effective pedagogical tools and techniques. And while an occasional inquirer might push for making education public, to the dismay of his colleagues, learning would be thought of as most properly private, and so the need for privacy would be taken as a given, rather than being taken as a historical development. Notice now how a Foucauldian critique of the imagined culture's construal of education would proceed. First it would stress the inevitability of learning in all sorts of contexts, and so the artificiality of restricting certain forms of education to the private realm. A Foucauldian critic would point out at length and in detail how even the most trivial encounter with another person or persons results in alteration or acquisition of belief, and so in learning. He would also point out that by far the bulk of what we do and learn is determined or influenced by others. The critic would then stress that since education is, in effect, ubiquitous, and its subjects infused with others' thought and action, there cannot in fact be wholly private learning. The critic might then explore the culture's history and show how early disastrous efforts at educational indoctrination drove their predecessors to protect the educational process by making it private, perhaps on the grounds that books and films are more easily censored and controlled than the activities of teachers. The critic would inventory the historical factors which made education seem ideally private, thereby showing that there is nothing inherently ideally private about learning or belief alteration and acquisition because the reasons for thinking cognitive change to be inherently ideally private are historical. We can imagine the culture in question being scandalized by a book titled not *The History of Sexuality* but rather *The Public Nature of Education.*

The foregoing example helps to clarify how Foucault argues that our present conception of sexuality is a historical product, a construct. But remember that Foucault is not just saying that sexuality is a social construct. If he were, our interest in his work would be interest in a basically sociological contribution. Foucault's work on sexuality—or on the clinic or the prison—goes beyond sociology because each of his case studies reflects a particular, very widespread conception of both the nature of the relevant object of intellectual inquiry and of intellectual inquiry itself. The crucial point of each of the Foucauldian case studies is that our discourses and practices produce what we then inquire into, and the implication with respect to philosophy is that philosophy cannot be a special mode of knowledge and inquiry just to the extent that history encompasses philosophy. Philosophical methods and problems are as historical as any. For Foucault, then, productive philosophical reflection on intellectual inquiry is basically an attempt to realize and appreciate how we have convinced ourselves of something. And if our history had been different, our convictions would also be different. Such reflection involves getting clear not only on the subject matter which concerns us, but on our methods of inquiry and how they, together with our practices, generate the subject matter in question.

Clearly this conception of philosophy and of intellectual inquiry would have been unthinkable for Descartes. The first idea he would have rejected out of hand is that there is no way to finally say we are right or wrong about something, that correctness is always a function of historically determined standards. Descartes could not accept the idea that there are no correctness criteria which are external to and independent of our discourses and practices. This point is so central that it bears restatement: what Foucault insists on, and what Descartes would have thought mad, is that there is nothing objective against which we can measure either our methods of inquiry or the conclusions we reach. This is the point made in the above quotation from Rorty: there are no criteria that we have not created in the course of creating our practices; there is no standard of rationality that is not an appeal to the criteria we have ourselves established. The trouble is that we invariably objectify the criteria we create; we project the standards we establish onto a world we take as unaffected by our cognitive activity. Then we read back those standards into that cognitive activity as if they were part of nature and not our own creations.

It may now be better appreciated that, as mentioned earlier, for Foucault there is no possibility of gaining intellectual freedom, of shedding all our self-imposed conceptions and criteria. As thinkers and agents we necessarily act on the basis of various conceptions and engage in various practices, and both generate criteria for their own measurement. The best we can hope for is to trade unproductive ones for productive ones. It is a pious dream to think that the truth can make us free. Foucauldian truth is itself a constraint; it precludes the sort of freedom we could not in any case achieve or even understand. Objective truth is simply not available, for it is no more than what we take to be the case, what we consider normal and natural. In the case of sexuality, for example, we have for centuries taken paired heterosexual unions as normal and deemed any other arrangement as unnatural. Because of the nature of procreation, we see heterosexual pairing as in the order of things. For a very long time this was the truth. But we have begun to understand that all we need to do is imagine a successful social system which organizes genders differently to realize that heterosexual pairing is only one of various possible arrangements which may be productive in various ways beyond sheer procreation. We have begun to understand what E. O. Wilson stresses in *On Human Nature*, namely, that sex is as much a bonding device as it is a procreative one. (Wilson, 1978:142) And such bonding may vary from culture to culture depending on their needs and values, and as how they have determined the truth of their sexuality.

When we begin to appreciate the radical nature and implications of Foucault's work, it becomes tempting to read him as if his aim were only to shake our intellectual complacency, and that the challenge his work poses can be met within traditional methodologies. This is the view of Charles Taylor, and it is an appealing one. (Taylor, 1987) But Foucault's aim is to have us reconceive those methodologies themselves. Foucault wants us to see that the very possibility of developing the alternatives he offers manifests not just the chance that we may have got things wrong and should reconsider, but that there simply is *no way* to get things finally right or wrong. His is not merely a provocative counterpoint to the Cartesian quest for certainty; it is a total rejection of it and everything it presupposes.

To capture the nature of Foucault's vision, many follow his own practice and characterize that vision by saying that Foucault thinks all truth is political. This can be read in various ways, the most likely of which is to say that it means anything we judge to be true is judged so because of operant interests and objectives. The rejection of the claim that sexuality has been repressed since the Victorian Age is, then, the claim that the accepted truth of repressed sexuality is a product of a number of intersecting power-relations which, for varied reasons, put a premium on controlling sexuality in several ways. This is obviously a point at which Foucault is again very close to feminist thinking. The way he describes the discourses and technologies of sexuality as casting women in the role of primarily sexual and emotional beings, and how women are then made to accept themselves as sexual subjects of a determinate sort, coincides with how feminists describe women as having come to be controlled in essentially political ways. All that is missing, as far as feminists are concerned, is attribution of the discourses and technologies in question, and the resulting control, to men as flowing from their political interests and objectives. However, Foucault's idea of power does not allow that, which is why many feminists argue that his notion of power is inadequate to account for the persistent domination of women. (Diamond and Quinby, 1988) But the reason should be clear by now: Foucault is not willing to identify power with domination. While Foucault can productively describe the genealogy of the status of women in our culture, he cannot limit power to the control men may impose on women by casting women as the subjects described in *The History of Sexuality*. What Foucault wants is for us to understand that what he describes as power is more an environment for human relations than a particular relation of dominance between even such extensive groups as men and women. The truth of sexuality, then, is political at a broader level even than that at which two halves of the human race are the protagonists.

To return to the main point, in presenting his case of how our discourses and practices actually constitute and reveal extensive interest in sexuality instead of its repression, Foucault is showing us how a different historical narrative supports an equally or more forceful political truth: that sexuality was enhanced and embellished and made the subject of obsessive concern. But whether enhanced *or* repressed, sexuality is a product of power-relations; it is not a true state of affairs separate from its interpretations and which may be clearly or distortedly perceived in those interpretations.

To close this section we can go a little beyond Foucault's concern with power to make a point that, while it raises difficult questions and invites much more discussion of his views, may shed light on what has been said about Foucault's work. Less than two years before his then unforeseen early death, Foucault said in an interview that the real goal of his work

> during the last 20 years . . . has not been to analyze the phenomena of power. . . . My objective, instead, has been to create a history of the different modes by which . . . human beings are made subjects. My work has dealt with three modes of objectification which transform human beings into subjects. The first is the modes of inquiry which try to give themselves the status of sciences. . . . [Second,] the objectivizing of the subject . . . [where the] . . . subject is either divided inside himself or divided from others. Examples are the mad and the sane, the sick and the healthy, the criminals and the "good boys." Finally, the way a human being turns him- or herself into a subject. Thus it is not power, but the subject, which is the general theme of my research. (Dreyfus and Rabinow, 1983:208–09)

What Foucault claims here is, in a way, inevitable, because the point of understanding power is to understand how it shapes human beings, and the primary way it does that is to make them subjects of a certain sort. Since power is not a *force*, once we understand how persons become subjects of specific sorts, we understand how their actions are constrained, how they are governed. And that is to understand everything, because we are no longer beings coerced by externalities needing investigation; we are beings governed by internalized norms of our own making. But we must be careful. For Foucault to say we are beings of any sort is not to suggest more than that we are ourselves products of our discourses, practices and history. Foucault did not believe in a Cartesian self; he believed that "the individual is not a pre-given entity. . . . The individual . . . is the product of a relation of power exercised over bodies, multiplicities, movements, desires, forces." (Foucault, 1980b:73–4) If it is hard for either the novice or the professional philosopher to accept that truth is a product of power, how much harder to accept that the person is too. But if we balk here, we will have missed most of the point of Foucault's work. Foucault is not just a constructivist with respect to sexuality; he is not even just a constructivist with respect to truth and knowledge; he is a constructivist with respect to what each of us is as a sexual being, a knower and an inquirer. What each of us is is what our activities and our history have made us:

> The individual is not to be conceived as a sort of elementary nucleus . . . on which power comes to fasten or against which it happens to strike. . . . In fact, it is already one of the prime effects of power that certain bodies, certain gestures, certain discourses, certain desires, come to be identified and constituted as individuals. The individual is an effect of power, and at the same time . . . it is the element of its articulation. The individual which power has constituted is at the same time its vehicle. (Foucault, 1980b:98)

We are here a very long way indeed from Descartes's starting point: an autonomous ego capable of coolly reflecting on its nature and beliefs.

CONCLUSION

As was made clear in the Introduction, this book is far from being an orthodox introduction to philosophy. What the book offers is a "jump start" in philosophy for those new to it, and for others a reminder of what is central to the tradition and a characterization of what most directly challenges that tradition. By providing some understanding of the extremes of how truth and knowledge may be conceived, the book sketches the outer limits within which debate about philosophizing and intellectual inquiry occurs. In the case of Descartes, the book lays out much that its readers will have internalized and assimilated—and perhaps reflected upon—as they were educated, and so it objectifies what they understand too well. In the case of Foucault, the book lays out what is most at odds with the tradition, and so objectifies what its readers, novices and experts alike, need to understand better. Admittedly, in some cases, things may be the other way around, in that some readers will be better versed in Foucauldian thought than in the Cartesian tradition. But in our time the Cartesian tradition is still dominant and the Foucauldian too novel, which means that regardless of conscious commitments to a Foucauldian perspective, much of a reader's "mind-set" almost certainly will be Cartesian in character. But whichever perspective is favored, consciously or otherwise, the point here has been to present as pointedly as possible the *contrast* between these extreme alternatives.

Unfortunately, in spite of the repetition and my efforts to state complex positions as clearly and accessibly as possible, misunderstandings and prejudiced interpretations are bound to occur. Along with careful reading and extensive discussion of the subject matter, the best defense against unproductive interpretations is reiterated reading. Each time a text is read different things emerge as notable, and this enables comparison of varying interpretations, and so facilitates recognition of interpretive problems. It would be extremely useful to be able to list likely interpretive difficulties, but it is actually quite difficult to successfully anticipate and/or describe philosophical misunderstanding. The reason is that all too often these misunderstandings are due more to lack of appreciation of the scope, nature and abstractness of something than to simple error or distortion. Differently put, readers more often fail to see the implications of a point or thesis than they simply misconstrue the thesis or point. As should be evident, say from the easy slide in the second meditation from Descartes's awareness of his own thought to his claim that he is a *thing* (a mind) that thinks, philosophical claims can be packed into very mundane and unexceptional remarks. And this sort of error can be compounded, in that one common sort of philosophical misunderstanding has to do with failing to appreciate not just the import of particular claims but the nature of a philosophical project.

Many traditionally oriented readers of Foucault assume that he concentrates on sexuality because sexuality is something that interests most people, and that he has a thesis which he only illustrates by discussing sexuality. They fail to see that this assumption not only grants to sexuality just the status that Foucault is concerned to question, but also that it misconceives his project because the assumption entails that Foucault is a theoretician, and that what he calls genealogy is only a means to an end. In this way they fail to see the *exhaustiveness* of genealogy, and hence the kind of understanding that Foucault offers. A consequence of this misunderstanding is that the same people then continue to conceive of truth as liberating, and to think that Foucault is making truth-claims, though in an eccentric way. Another example of misunderstanding of this order, alluded to before, is that many read and dismiss Foucault as a "mere" relativist. They fail to appreciate that to be a relativist in the traditional philosophical sense one has to accept the coherence of the objectivistic/relativistic distinction, and that Foucault does not do so, since he sees that very distinction as a product of a particular unproductive discourse.

There are also more routine misunderstandings. One, for instance, has to do with getting so caught up in the details of a philosophical project that the proper degree of abstractness of a claim or thesis is lost to sight. In the case of Foucault, too many who read *The History of Sexuality* miss the implications with respect to truth and knowledge because they concentrate overmuch on what is said about sexuality. This is perhaps most evident, not in the work of philosophers or intellectual historians, but in the work of more popular commentators who view Foucault as a social critic mainly concerned to warn against the mechanics of contemporary manipulative techniques. While these commentators often make productive use of Foucault's work, they usually miss the episte- mological and more broadly philosophical implications of that work. (Franklin, 1990) This latter misunderstanding is likelier to occur in connection with Foucault than with Descartes, but there are other sorts of misunderstanding of which the opposite is true. For instance, if one's inclination is to see Descartes through Fou- cauldian glasses, it is necessary to work very hard to avoid a kind of historical fallacy, namely, thinking that the lapse of nearly four hundred years has somehow antiquated Descartes's views and less- ened the seriousness of his questions. This is to see philosophical issues as too much the products of their time, and would be not only to underestimate the importance of Cartesian questions, but also to take too facile and superficial a position regarding Foucault, because it would be to reject Cartesian questions as *simply* those of another time, without real understanding of how those questions arose in their time, and which of their causes or conditions for being might still exist.

But if the contrast between Descartes and Foucault has been drawn, and the reader is now on guard against shallow interpre- tation, what more might be said? There can be little hope of con- cluding by offering useful further summation of what has already been summarized in our consideration of Descartes's *Meditations* and Foucault's *The History of Sexuality*. Additionally, our comparison of their two radically opposed philosophical positions resists further summation because each position excludes some of the principles which would serve as organizing devices for facilitating summation of the other position. But no further summary is needed; the point of the exercise was to expose the reader to the most extreme al- ternatives available with respect to conceptions of knowledge and truth, and the central points defining those conceptions have been adequately stressed. Throughout I have risked tediousness by re- peating these central points numerous times and from different perspectives to insure that they were not only understood, but that their implications were appreciated. Of these central points, the one most often repeated was how intellectual inquiry for Descartes was a *search* while for Foucault it was a *constructive* exercise, how knowledge was for Descartes hard-won awareness of objective truth while for Foucault knowledge was the production of truth. This is how for Descartes truth was that which awaits discovery and which, once discovered, cannot be confused or mistaken, and how for Foucault truth was whatever power says it is, and as such is constantly changing radically or undergoing piecemeal adjustment. For Descartes, then, the self was the utterly unquestionable starting point for philosophizing, that one absolutely certain existent awareness of which can ground all knowledge, while for Foucault the self was what history and practice determine it to be, and even the self-awareness Descartes took so seriously is a function of operant presuppositions and interpretive inclinations. As I said earlier, had Descartes read Foucault he would have thought Foucault crazy, because Descartes would have taken Foucault to be denying what is most obvious. In like manner, having read Descartes, Foucault must have thought him intellectually naive to place such trust on his internal perceptions and to have believed there is an essential ego independent of its beliefs and practices. We have here an opposition between conception of ourselves as autonomous investigators able to apply an inviolable rationality to all we encounter, and of ourselves as basically self-deceived products of blind and usually contrary influences. But it is an opposition that may largely elude us. As Foucault might warn, it is an opposition so deep and crucial that when we try to confront it in a book like this, it may masquerade as an academic problem; it may present itself to us as clear at an abstract level, while its real bulk slips iceberg-like past us. It would be a good way to conclude, then, to come again at this opposition in still another way.

This book, in being about two diametrically opposed and mutually exclusive philosophical perspectives or stances, poses the inescapable and intellectually pressing question of which perspective or stance you might endorse. And the choices seem limited; given the nature of Descartes's and Foucault's views, it is difficult to see what could constitute a *third* alternative. But it may be that while the foregoing chapters have provided a general understanding of the Cartesian and Foucauldian perspectives, you feel less than comfortable with respect to how the contrast between Descartes's and Foucault's conceptions of truth and knowledge actually applies to specific issues. Perhaps the best way to look again at the Cartesian/

Foucauldian opposition would be to illustrate the clash between the Platonic/Cartesian/Kantian tradition and postmodern rejection of it. The most effective way to do so it to show how a contemporary critic of the tradition, other than Foucault, approaches a particular, though admittedly very broad, traditional philosophical conception and the problems it generates, and attempts to show how that conception is determined by problematic presuppositions. The critic's objective in identifying those presuppositions is to undermine, if not refute, that conception, and thereby to dissolve rather than resolve the problems to which that conception gives rise.

By now it should be clear how the rise of traditional epistemology was largely a consequence of Descartes's skeptical point of departure. Whatever Descartes may have achieved, what he did not achieve was what he set out to do in the *Meditations*, which was to wholly answer the questions raised by his dream and evil-genius devices and so establish knowledge on indubitable foundations. The Cartesian legacy, then, is the continuing need to refute skepticism. If we return to Peirce's rejection of Cartesian epistemology, we will recall that Peirce's main objection was precisely to Descartes's skeptical point of departure. But while Peirce's critical points are persuasive, they lack the power of postmodern critiques because they offer little by way of clarification of what initially enabled, and in a sense forced, Descartes to proceed as he did. In a fairly straightforward way, Peirce was too committed to Kantian principles and methodology; he was himself too much a modern philosopher to have delved deeply enough into what underlay Descartes's project and enabled his point of departure. Peirce begins by taking Descartes's position as a philosophical one, a wrong-headed one, but nonetheless a position. Peirce then rejects *that* Descartes took an initially skeptical stance, but he is less concerned to understand and say *why* Descartes did so. In spite of his pragmatism and his awareness that he and his peers were initiating new ways of philosophizing, it is very likely that Peirce's Kantian inclination insured that he was still of the opinion that historical factors were both isolable and of essentially secondary importance with respect to philosophical theses. He would most probably not have considered historical factors as *directly* relevant to philosophical claims, and so would not have considered them capable of justifying dismissal of those claims. Like some contemporaries, Peirce felt that the skeptic had to be *answered*, not ignored.

In contrast to Peirce and others who challenged Descartes more or less on Descartes's own terms, Rorty, perhaps North America's leading postmodern philosopher, has clarified for us that Cartesian skepticism was not a then novel and *legitimate* approach to philosophical issues, but rather was something made possible and in effect inevitable by a sequence of misconceptions. Rorty condenses these misconceptions into what was touched on at the end of Part I and which he dubs a "representationalist" view of thought and awareness. The burden of this characterization is that once we understand how skepticism, and so epistemology, are products of an inherently unworkable view of the mind, knowledge and truth, we will dismiss them as not worth our time.

Rorty articulates the key notion of Platonic/Cartesian thinking as a juxtaposition of us, as aware subjects, to an autonomous and determinate world. The central belief in this notion is that the autonomous and determinate world is accessible to us, is presented to us as a complex object, only *indirectly*. We, as aware subjects, have access to the world only through ideational facsimiles of that world: in short, we are aware of the world solely through representations of the world which occur in our minds. From this everything else follows, particularly the great epistemological project of verifying or confirming that those representations in our minds are *accurate* representations of the world, that they are faithful portraits at least of bits of the world. Rorty's challenge to Cartesianism, then, is not just another move within the epistemological tradition; it is an attempt to undermine that entire tradition by revealing how it arises from a deep misconception. Rorty's maneuver here is comparable to Foucault's rejection of the repressive hypothesis through demonstration that the repression of sexuality is illusory and that in fact the activities which allegedly comprised the repression of sexuality actually served to greatly augment interest in and treatment of sexuality.

Rorty plays on the metaphor of mirroring to characterize the Cartesian conception of mind as one of the mind or awareness being "a mirror of nature," and so as something *inherently* detached from the world. This metaphor nicely captures what is essential to traditional epistemology: the mind is capable of mirroring the world; that is what awareness of the world *is*. The only question, then, is whether our mental mirror-image is faithful to what it reflects. As we saw with Descartes, our internal mirrorings are not to be thought of as perfectly accurate to their originals, but they can be more or less so, at least to the extent of either constituting knowledge of the world or illusion. Both Plato and Descartes understood that mental mirrorings cannot be *exact* copies, but neither offered a sufficiently sophisticated account of just how mental mirroring can be accurate in spite of not being capable of exact reproduction. Locke added the notion that there was a difference between "primary" qualities or properties, which characterize the things in the world in themselves, and "secondary" qualities or properties, which are features of how we experience the world. But as Berkeley later demonstrated, Locke's distinction could not be made out rigorously and in effect produced more problems than it solved. In short, primary qualities could be argued to be reducible to secondary or redundant qualities. What Kant added to Plato's and Descartes's basic mirroring notion was that however the world may be *in itself*, we can know it, we can have ideas which represent it, only within the confines of certain modes of thought, certain categories, which take what impinges on us and organize and shape it into a coherent picture of the world. Rather than two sorts of properties, then, the distinction was to be drawn between an *unknowable* world in itself and how we represent that world, including the apparently most basic properties we deem it to have, such as temporality, spatiality and causality. That is, even time, space and causal connection were supposed to be modes or aspects of how we represent the world, rather than being modes or aspects of the world itself. As for how the world itself may be, that was literally unthinkable and the notion supposedly introduced only for the sake of contrast.

But Kant's enhancement of the original conception, his making our subjectivity a more active one by giving the mind a configuring role with respect to awareness, really changed nothing in the basic representationalist conception. The basic idea is still that we (may) know something about what is "out there" only by having replicas "in here." In fact, Kant's enhancement really made things worse, because it led to the suspicion that different subjects might configure the world differently, but still in successful and so undetectably diverse ways. This meant there might be as many *experienced* worlds as there are subjects, and that all or many of these experienced worlds might still serve to enable their subjects to survive and even to flourish, never knowing whether their fellows share any part of their experienced environments.

A somewhat pejorative but very effective characterization of the representationalist conception of mind or knowledge and awareness was provided by W. V. O. Quine (1908–), who called this conception "the idea idea." (Quine, 1981:68) Quine's point is that Plato, Descartes and Kant shared the idea that awareness is always of ideas—however ideas may be defined or explained. The phrase might easily have been Nietzsche's, whose opposition to the Platonic tradition was in no small part defined by his rejection of what Quine would later call the idea idea. But as noted in the Introduction, while extremely persuasive to many, Nietzsche's criticism of the tradition was too insouciant for most professional philosophers. Perhaps the earliest effective rejection of the idea idea is in the work of Peirce and particularly of John Dewey (1859–1952), who argued vehemently against the view that awareness is constituted by a sequence of ideas which the mind apprehends directly and which, as the effects of what is in the world, yield our only knowledge of the world.

Generally, the problem with the idea idea which Rorty is concerned to highlight is that once awareness is understood as *mediated* by representations, we are isolated as subjects by an unbridgeable gulf which is opened between us and the world. In other words, as conscious subjects we are rendered isolated Cartesian non-extended points of awareness, and the world is reciprocally rendered an inaccessible mystery of which we have only second-hand cognizance. This is why Gadamer's rejection of the reliability of internal reflection, mentioned earlier, is so telling a blow to the Cartesian tradition. Once we are isolated as Cartesian subjects, the only source of knowledge is what is given to us in what Descartes called a clear and distinct way. This means that if we impugn reasoned and minimal internal reflection, if we dare think, as do Gadamer and Foucault, that even the simplest things that appear one or another way to us may do so because of our histories and inclinations, we must either abandon ourselves to total isolation and lack of knowledge or reconceive how we are subjects. As has been pointed out several times, the result of this conception of ourselves as isolated, dimensionless subjects is the entire tradition of Cartesian philosophy, which has at its heart the epistemological problem of determining whether and how we can *trust* our ideas. But that problem is a philosophical one; there is a more pervasive and subtle result of what Rorty calls representationalism, which is the general conception of intellectual inquiry as discernment of elusive truth. Scientists are then thought of as wresting truths from nature; historians as reconstructing objective accounts of events from diverse stories; medical researchers as divining causes and effects from a welter of confusing symptoms, and so on. Given the view that inquiry is a matter of somehow acquiring the most faithful representations possible, when there is disagreement or problems arise in inquiry, the assumption will be that the truth has not yet been found.

Additionally, in the foregoing view of inquiry, all that goes into making something an interest, into making something a question, and into making something else an answer to a question, is discarded as extraneous, as a bar to objectivity, and so to the discovery of truth. Cultural and theoretical commitments are supposedly things to be *overcome*, in the sense that they are looked on as biases or prejudices, as complications and obfuscations, and not integral to inquiry and its resolution. The ideal is seen as unbiased and objective inquirers seeking truth without their own interests and other background factors coloring the questions they ask or the answers nature yields. But this is to imagine that it is possible to achieve description of the world from no particular perspective, from a God's-eye view. It is to imagine that not only are we aware of the world in virtue of internal representations, but that those representations can be as interest- and value-neutral as their originals in the world are, as objects themselves are. Another way of putting this point is to say that in the representationalist view of awareness and knowledge, the fundamental case is one of the formation of internal representations as determined purely by their external causes. What goes wrong is that either we employ these representations hastily or otherwise ineffectively, or we distort them in complicated ways because of our own beliefs and expectations. Supposedly what the perspicacious inquirer does is to strip away distorting influences and work with representations in their purest form. Only then can inquirers achieve sound conclusions not only about representations but, indirectly, about their external originals, and so only then can we gain knowledge.

What is important to appreciate in all this is that what the traditionalist or modern philosopher sees as the conditions of philosophical inquiry, namely, objectivity and sound representational data, are seen by the postmodern critic as the main source of the problems which that inquiry then addresses and which therefore determine the tradition. Initially, the critic is less concerned about what traditional inquirers think they must be objective about, than with the idea that there *can* be objective inquiry and objectively attended-to data. The critic sees this notion of a required objectivity as flowing from the very conception of "data" as internal representations, for once something *is* deemed a representation, it must be thought *accurate* if it is to be worth anything. For the contemporary critic, then, the problems which claim the efforts of the modern philosopher are less problems than they are symptoms of misconception. Rather than calling for solutions, what these problems do is pose questions about how they came to be considered parts of the general philosophical enterprise.

As a last word I offer this caution: all of the foregoing tends to paint a picture of postmodern philosophers as defiant iconoclasts and even as heroic, and of modern philosophers as at best caught in a web of misconception from within which they dogmatically shape and control intellectual inquiry, if not culture itself. This is a picture which, at least generally, appeals to contemporary students, and which perhaps too quickly prompts rejection and even scorn from their professors. The "subtext" of my presentation of the contrast between Descartes and Foucault is that the novice should take seriously the virtues and power of the modern perspective, and that the traditionally more knowledgeable should do the same with respect to the postmodern perspective. The real challenge facing philosophy in our time is how to somehow combine the best elements of both the modern and postmodern perspectives. The reason this challenge is enormous is that these perspectives seem to be totally exclusive of one another, because they demand irreconcilable conceptions of truth and knowledge and intellectual inquiry itself. Perhaps this is why we have seen a resurgence of pragmatism in recent years. (Rorty, 1982) Perhaps we have no option but to work with flexible notions of what is most definitive of rational thought and so should be wholly determinate and ungiving. But it is very hard to see how truth and knowledge could be anything but objective and absolute without then being entirely products of history. Happily, it is not my burden to offer solutions. My task has been only to lay out as clearly and succinctly as possible the nature of the most divergent options on the issue of the nature of truth and knowledge.

GLOSSARY

ANTIEPISTEMOLOGY, ANTIEPISTEMOLOGIST: see EPISTEMOL-
OGY.

A PRIORI: that which can be known prior to or without the need of
experience. For example, it is *a priori* that the internal angles of a triangle
equal 180 degrees. One does not need to go about measuring triangles to
know this is true. Note that empiricists identify the *a priori* and the analytic,
while rationalists think them different. In other words, empiricists think
that analytic expressions are necessarily true (or necessarily false) by definition. Rationalists believe some may be true or false in ways not dependent
on definitions—for instance, because of the necessity of a mode of representation.

A POSTERIORI: that which cannot be know prior to or without experience of the world.

ANALYTIC: said of an expression the truth (or falsity) of which depends
only on the meaning of the terms used. In Kantian terms, these expressions
are described as ones where the subject "contains" the predicate in the
sense that all we need to do to establish truth or falsity is carefully analyze
the sense of the subject. Examples range from evident identity statements
such as "A is A" to statements like "All bachelors are unmarried men."

BEHAVIORISM: the view that our talk about minds is exhaustively
reducible to talk about verbal or bodily behavior.

CLARITY; DISTINCTNESS: These are Descartes's qualifiers for ideas
that present themselves to the mind in a perfectly transparent way, i.e.,

involving no confusion or ambiguity, and wholly contained, i.e., in themselves and not as related to or dependent on other ideas.

CONCEPT: essentially a recognitional capacity. Having the concept of red means being able to pick out something of a certain sort: i.e., something red. Often 'concept' is used—wrongly—as synonymous with 'idea'.

CONSTRUCTIVIST: one who believes that the objects of human knowledge are, at least in part and at least as present to us, determined by historical and psychological factors and so are conditioned by subjective elements belonging to their apprehension or mode of apprehension.

DETERMINISM: the view that everything that occurs is brought about by a sufficient cause and hence could not have been otherwise.

DECONSTRUCTION: this term is too widely used at present to allow for rigid definition. Basically it refers to the sort of critique practiced by Jacques Derrida which involves teasing out from any given position elements antithetical to that same position. Effectively the objective is to show any and all positions to be no more than favored perspectives.

DISTINCTNESS: see CLARITY.

DUALISM: the view that there are two fundamentally different substances: mind or the mental and body or the material.

EMPIRICISM: basically the philosophical position that all knowledge derives from experience. Empiricism is best understood as the denial of the basic tenet of RATIONALISM, namely, that there is some knowledge that derives from reason alone and which is independent of experience.

EPISTEMOLOGY: the theory of knowledge, which inquires into what can be known, with what degree of certainty and under what conditions; that central area of philosophy concerned with the nature and justification of knowledge claims. Epistemologists are concerned to "ground" human knowledge in either self-verifying truths or an experiential "given." An antiepistemologist is one who believes that human knowledge cannot be justified beyond consensus, general effectiveness or pragmatic value, and practice.

ETHICS: that part of value-theory, which includes aesthetics, having to do with the study of the nature and justification of judgments about right and wrong conduct. Note: in our culture ethics is often confused with the religious, or at least seen as entailing or entailed by the religious. While religious views invariably entail or involve ethical views, the reverse is not the case, in spite of the common view. One need not be religious to be ethical, and an ethic or moral code can be quite independent of any religious notion. 'Ethics' and 'ethical' are usually used synonymously with 'morality' and 'moral'. Some use 'ethics' and 'ethical' to refer to what is universally correct with respect to conduct, and 'morality' and 'moral' to refer to what a particular culture considers to be ethical.

EXISTENTIALISM: the position, most notably that of Jean-Paul Sartre, which maintains that existence precedes essence. In other words, it is a denial of essences and an affirmation of the constitutive role of practice and the responsibility of the individual for self-determination. Usually existentialism is maintained as an ethical position. A looser, more popular sense is that having to do with the isolation of the individual and the individual's confrontation of pressing but ambiguous situations.

GENEALOGICAL: that which pertains to GENEALOGY.

GENEALOGY: a term borrowed from ordinary usage and used, notably by Nietzsche and Foucault, to designate the careful and precise study and articulation of the specific history of an institution, idea or term. Also the practice of compiling genealogies.

INTUITION: though Kant's use of 'intuition' is more like our use of 'sense' or even 'experience', earlier philosophers like Descartes used 'intuition' to refer to direct awareness of truth without need of inference or analysis. Usually 'intuition' is used with respect to claimed direct awareness of ethical value.

METAPHYSICAL: that which pertains to metaphysics, as in 'metaphysical claim' or 'metaphysical element'.

METAPHYSICS: that part of philosophical inquiry and speculation that concerns itself with ultimate reality. See ONTOLOGY.

METHODOLOGICAL DOUBT: doubt assumed for the purpose of proving whatever is doubted, a device used to strategically impugn what might otherwise not be questioned.

METHODOLOGY: a rule-governed procedure or set of procedures for dealing with a problematic matter.

OBJECTIVIST: one who believes the objects of knowledge to be free of subjective components contributed by the knower and so not conditioned by psychological or historical factors or other elements having to do with their apprehension or mode of apprehension.

ONTOLOGY: the subdiscipline in philosophy which deals with being as such; with what is and what it is to be. Ontological questions deal with the ultimate and/or relative nature of the subjects of our discourse: i.e., minds, material objects, experiences.

POSTMODERN: while the term originally applied to art, it is now used to mean intellectual methods, objectives, values, topics, and interests which share the rejection of the Enlightenment assumption of objective truth and the possibility of real, cumulative progress in inquiry.

PRIMARY QUALITY: supposedly, the qualities or properties objects in the world actually have in the sense of not being perception-dependent, such as their mass, size, figure and number. See SECONDARY QUALITY.

PROPOSITION: for some, simply a thought or the content of thought; that which can be thought or articulated in a spoken or written sentence. The proposition is what is translated from, say, an English sentence to a French sentence. The proposition is what is true or false. The proposition is what is said in a sentence, so: "The sentence 'The cat is sleeping' says the same as the Spanish sentence 'El gato duerme'." With respect to belief, the proposition is what is believed. Some use 'proposition' more or less synonymously with 'sentence'.

RATIONAL: that which is properly reasoned; also that which satisfies criteria having to do with logical progression and validity. The common sense in which we speak of someone being "rational," as opposed to mad or deranged, derives from the philosophical sense that what distinguishes us is that we reason as opposed to only respond to stimuli or emotional prompting.

RATIONALISM: the philosophical position that at least some knowledge derives from reason alone. As with EMPIRICISM, this position is best understood in terms of its opposite: as the stance opposite to the claim that knowledge derives solely from experience.

REASON: narrowly, our ability to establish and implement suitable means-to-ends measures to attain our goals; more broadly, the ability to think coherently and to think reflectively or in a self-aware mode.

RELATIVISM: the view that because there are no objective standards, truth- and value-judgments are always relative to cultural, group, or personal preferences. This is sometimes put provocatively as the view that any position or claim is as good as any other.

SECONDARY QUALITY: supposedly a quality or property attributed to an object only because of the action of that object on a percipient: specifically, taste, color, odor, feel and sound.

SELF-EVIDENT: that the truth (or falsity) of which is present in the very thought of it, as in the self-evidency of the truth of 'A = A' or the self-evident falsity of 'squared circle'. Usually 'self-evident' is applied to principles, such as the principle of noncontradiction.

SENSES: our sensory apparatus. More importantly, knowledge acquired through the senses is usually contrasted, in philosophy, with knowledge acquired through intuition or rational inference or claimed to be part and parcel of being rational.

STRUCTURALISM: generally, the view that observable phenomena, for instance human behavior or language, are a function of underlying structures or systems. The term most often applies to linguistics, but for our purposes what is important is the postulation of theoretically discernible formations of elements underlying thought, speech and action.

SUBSTANCE: that which exists independently of all else—as opposed to a property, which must inhere in a substance or substantial thing.

SUFFICIENT CAUSE/SUFFICIENT CONDITION: usually contrasted with necessary cause/condition. A sufficient cause/condition is or would be all that is or would be needed for something to happen: it is sufficient that the powder in a shell explode for the bullet to be fired, while it is a necessary but not sufficient cause/condition of the bullet's being fired that the powder be dry.

SYNTHETIC: said of sentences, propositions or judgments, and usually defined in Kant's terms as a sentence, proposition or judgment in which the predicate adds new information to the subject. In practice synthetic sentences, propositions, and judgments are experience-based, as opposed to ANALYTIC ones, where the predicate is said to be "contained" in the subject and hence adds no new information to what is understood about the subject. ANALYTIC sentences, propositions and judgments are true or false on the basis of definition or, as some contend, on the basis of meaning. Against this, synthetic ones are true or false on the basis of how we discern the world to be.

THEOLOGY: that part of human inquiry concerned with determining, to the best extent possible, the nature of God.

TRUTH: this is a tough one, because the main issue is whether truth admits of definition, and if so, of what sort of theoretical definition: for example, as the "correspondence" of sentences to facts ("Correspondence theory"), or as the "coherence" among sentences ("Coherence theory"). The contemporary critics of Cartesian philosophizing insist that truth does not admit of theoretical definition, and that to call a sentence "true" is only to make a certain kind of endorsement in language. For discussion of Descartes's views, take "truth" to be correspondence of sentences to facts or to "how the world is."

VERIFICATION: as used in philosophy, the establishing of the truth or falsity of some claim or belief by appealing to actual or at least possible sense experience. "Verificationism" is, roughly, the view that for claims to be meaningful they must be confirmable by actual or possible experience. Verificationists oppose metaphysical speculation, claiming that anything not verifiable by experience is literally meaningless and at most an emotive expression of a complex sort.

BIBLIOGRAPHY

Allen, Barry (1991). "Government in Foucault." *Canadian Journal of Philosophy*, 21(4):421–40.

Baynes, Kenneth, James Bohman, and Thomas McCarthy, eds. (1987). *After Philosophy: End or Transformation*. Cambridge, Mass.: MIT Press.

Bernauer, James, and David Rasmussen, eds. (1988). *The Final Foucault*. Cambridge, Mass.: MIT Press.

Buchler, J., ed. (1955). *Philosophical Writings of Peirce*. New York: Dover Publications.

Cervantes, Miguel de (1963). *Don Quixote*. Baltimore: Penguin.

Code, Lorraine (1987). *Epistemic Responsibility*. Hanover: Brown University Press (University Presses of New England).

Cornford, Francis (1957). *Plato's Theory of Knowledge*. New York: Bobbs-Merrill.

Cottingham, John, Robert Stoothoff and Dugald Murdoch (1985). *The Philosophical Writings of Descartes*. Cambridge: Cambridge University Press.

Davidson, Donald (1986). "A Coherence Theory of Truth and Knowledge." In Ernest LePore, ed. (1986), *Truth and Interpretation: Perspectives on the Philosophy of Donald Davidson*. New York: Blackwell, pp. 307–19.

Debus, A. G. (1978). *Man and Nature in the Renaissance*. Cambridge: Cambridge University Press.

Descartes, René. *Meditations on First Philosophy*. Laurence J. Lafleur, trans., Macmillan/Library of Liberal Arts, 1951 (1989); also Haldane and Ross, 1969.

————. *Discourse on Method*. Haldane and Ross, 1969.

————. *Arguments*. Haldane and Ross, 1969.

————. *Reply to Objections IV*. Haldane and Ross, 1969.

— BIBLIOGRAPHY —

Diamond, Irene, and Lee Quinby, eds., (1988). *Feminism and Foucault: Reflections on Resistance.* Boston: Northeastern University Press.

Dreyfus, Hubert, and Paul Rabinow (1983). *Michel Foucault: Beyond Structuralism and Hermeneutics.* With an Afterword by Michel Foucault. Brighton, Sussex: The Harvester Press.

Fox Keller, Evelyn (1985). *Reflections on Gender and Science.* New Haven: Yale University Press.

Foucault, Michel (1972). *The Archaeology of Knowledge.* Trans. A.M. Sheridan-Smith. New York: Harper and Row.

————. (1977). *Discipline and Punish.* Trans. Alan Sheridan New York: Pantheon.

————. (1980a). *The History of Sexuality* (Volume One). Trans. Robert Hurley. New York: Vintage.

————. (1980b). *Power/Knowledge: Selected Interviews and Other Writings.* Ed. Colin Gordon. New York: Pantheon.

————. (1986). *The Use of Pleasure.* Trans. Robert Hurley. New York: Vintage.

————. (1988). *The Care of the Self.* Trans. Robert Hurley. New York: Vintage.

————. (1989). *Foucault Live.* Trans. John Johnston, Sylvre Lotringer, ed. New York: Semiotext(e).

Franklin, Ursula (1990). *The Real World of Technology,* CBC Massey Lectures. Toronto: CBC Enterprises.

Guthrie, W. K. C. (1962). *The History of Greek Philosophy,* Vol. 1, Cambridge: Cambridge University Press.

Haldane, Elizabeth, and G. R. T. Ross (1969). *The Philosophical Works of Descartes,* Vols. I and II. Cambridge: Cambridge University Press.

Harding, Sandra, and Merrill Hintikka, eds. (1983). *Discovering Reality: Feminist Perspectives on Epistemology, Metaphysics, Methodology, and Philosophy of Science.* Dordrecht, Holland: Reidel.

Hoy, David Couzens (1986). *Foucault: A Critical Reader.* New York: Basil Blackwell.

Kemp-Smith, Norman (1958). *Descartes: Philosophical Writings.* New York: The Modern Library/Random House.

Kenny, Anthony, trans. and ed. (1970). *Descartes: Philosophical Letters.* Oxford: Clarendon Press.

Kiernan, Thomas P. (1962). *Aristotle Dictionary.* New York: Philosophical Library.

Kinsey, Alfred C. (1948–53). *Sexual Behavior in the Human Male* (1948) and *Sexual Behavior in the Human Female* (with W. B. Pomeroy and C. E. Martin, 1953). Philadelphia: Saunders.

Matson, W. I. (1965). *The Existence of God.* Ithaca: Cornell University Press.

Morris, John M. (1971). *Descartes Dictionary.* New York: Philosophical Library.

Nietzsche, Friedrich Wilhelm (1968). *Thus Spoke Zarathustra.* In Walter Kaufman (1968), *The Portable Nietzsche.* New York: Penguin.

O'Farrell, Clare (1989). *Foucault: Historian or Philosopher?* Houndmills: Macmillan.

Overstreet, Harry (1931). *The Enduring Quest.* New York: Norton.

Prado, C. G. (1986). *Rethinking How We Age: A New View of the Aging Mind,* Westport, Connecticut: Greenwood Press.

Quine, Willard Van Orman (1981). *Theories and Things.* Cambridge, Mass.: The Belknap Press of Harvard University Press.

Rorty, Richard (1991). *Essays on Heidegger and Others.* New York: Cambridge University Press.

————. (1982). *The Consequences of Pragmatism.* Minneapolis: University of Minnesota Press.

————. (1979). *Philosophy and the Mirror of Nature.* Princeton: Princeton University Press.

Snow, Charles Percy (1959). *Two Cultures.* Cambridge: Cambridge University Press.

Taylor, Charles (1986). "Foucault on Freedom and Truth." In Hoy (1986), pp. 69–102.

Taylor, Charles (1987). "Overcoming Epistemology." In Baynes (1987), pp. 464–85.

Wilson, E. O. (1978). *On Human Nature.* New York: Harvard University Press.

Wilson, Margaret (1978). *Descartes.* New York: Routledge.